Ottoman Decorative Arts

by
Ayşin YOLTAR-YILDIRIM

REPUBLIC OF TURKEY
MINISTRY OF CULTURE AND TOURISM PUBLICATIONS

General Directorate of Libraries and Publications
3227
Handbook Series
8

ISBN: 978-975-17-3446-4

www.kulturturizm.gov.tr
e-posta: yayimlar@kulturturizm.gov.tr

Yoltar Yıldırım, Ayşin

Ottoman Decorative Arts / Ayşin Yoltar-Yıldırım; Photos: Hadiye Cangökçe [...et al.] .- Ankara: Ministry of Culture and Tourism, 2009.

192 p.: col. ill.; 20 cm.- (Ministry of Culture and Tourism Publications; 3227. Handbook Series of General Directorate of Libraries and Publications: 8)

ISBN: 978-975-17-3446-4

I. title. II. Cangökçe, Hadiye. III. Series.
759.9561015

Printed by
CMS Tanıtım Hizmetleri Tic. Ltd. Şti.

Photographs
Hadiye Cangökçe, Ayşin Yoltar-Yıldırım (figs. 25, 36, 37, 73)
Photo credits: Topkapı Palace Museum, Istanbul Turkish and Islamic Arts Museum, Istanbul Archaeological Museum, Konya Mevlana Museum, Istanbul University Library, Nuruosmaniye Library, Sakıp Sabancı Museum

First Edition

Print run: 5000.

Printed in Ankara in 2009.

TABLE OF CONTENTS

Ottoman Decorative Arts

Note on Usage

Modern Turkish uses the Latin alphabet, modified to ensure that there is a separate letter for each main sound. The spelling thus aims at phonetic consistency. For Turkish artists, place names, publications and special terms this book employs modern Turkish spelling. Proper names have been kept in modern Turkish with one exception – İstanbul has been rendered with normal English spelling using I rather than İ unless it is part of a title. Consonants have more or less the same sound as in English, except for:

c like j in English

ç like ch in English

ğ the "soft g". Depending on the adjoining letters, this is dropped, pronounced like y in English, or treated as lengthening the preceding vowel.

ı is a back, close, unrounded vowel which does not exist in English, the nearest equivalent being the phantom vowel in the second syllable of rhythm.

ö like ö in German or eu in French peur

ş like sh in English

ü like ü in German or u in French

Chapter 1

Introduction

What are Ottoman decorative arts?

Ottoman art generally refers to the art produced under the Ottoman dynasty's rule from 1299 to 1923. Although the Ottoman Empire was centered in present day Turkey, mainly Istanbul, it spread to three continents at its zenith covering large geographic areas, roughly present day Turkey, Eastern Europe, Syria, Iraq, the Levant, Egypt and North Africa (Fig.1 Map of Ottoman Empire).

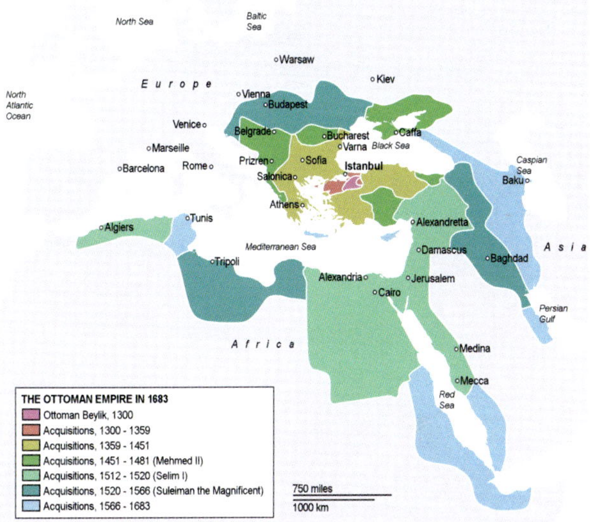

Fig.1 Map of Ottoman Empire (http://commons.wikimedia.org/wiki/File:OttomanEmpireIn1683.png)

Ottoman art also constitutes a branch of Islamic art, which can be studied from the late 7th century onwards until the modern era. Islamic art does not refer to the art of the Muslim faith, as in Buddhist art, but rather to the art produced in settings largely inhabited by Muslim populations. Islamic art, which was initially observed in Iraq, Syria and the Levant later spread to large geographic areas namely Iran, Afghanistan, Central Asia and India in the east, and Egypt, North Africa and Spain in the west, as Islam became a widely accepted religion far from its origin in Mecca and Medina in the Arabian Peninsula. Most of Islamic art concerns with secular subjects despite the term's religious suggestion. In all these lands Islamic art displays varying and unique qualities based on cultural, historical, political and social contexts although some general principals that reflect the sensitivities and preferences of a Muslim society can be found in all. Since Islamic art as a term covers a long time span and numerous geographic areas, studies focusing on a specific period or geography give us a chance to see the individual aspects of a culture within Islamic art. Ottoman art is an example of this phenomenon.

Ottoman decorative arts represent a large portion of Ottoman art. In Europe decorative arts usually refer to the decoration of functional objects as opposed to the nonutilitarian 'fine arts' of painting, large-scale sculpture and architecture. This division is generally not applicable to Islamic art (and Ottoman art). In Islamic art figural sculpture is rarely seen and figural painting is mostly reserved to ceramics and book illustrations. Instead Islamic art can be divided into two main areas: architecture and arts. Although the term decorative arts usually refers to the latter, architectural decoration can also be included when we talk about the surface decoration of buildings. Floral, calligraphic, geometric and to a certain degree figural decorations are ubiquitously found in Islamic art on almost any medium from metalwork to ceramics, turning everyday objects into fine art works.

This book surveys the general characteristics of Ottoman decorative arts on various and related media, such as, manuscripts and works on paper, tiles and ceramics, textiles and carpets, metalwork and jewelry, and woodwork. In the 19th and early 20th century under the influence of European art, painting and sculpture in the European manner were also practiced by the Ottomans. These have been excluded for consistency in the theme of the book. This book does consider architecture but mainly in terms of its decoration, which was predominantly in the form of tile and brushwork, particularly for the interior decoration of Ottoman architecture. Where relevant, decoration on stone or other materials on the exteriors of the buildings are also considered.

The book covers the time span of the Ottoman dynastic reign of six centuries (1299-1922) and explains the historical and cultural contexts in which Ottoman decorative arts were formed and flourished. It focuses on the design aspect of decorative arts and tries to show the range of styles that were common and also explains the underlying cause of the use of the same styles in various media. Since the Ottomans created a centralized empire, the arts produced under their patronage also reflect the impact of this system. Most of Ottoman art was created by artists who worked for the Ottoman court. The organization of the talented artists and craftsmen within the Ottoman court administration took place in the second half of the 15th century in the new capital of the Ottomans in Istanbul (formerly the Byzantine Constantinople). By the 16th century there were several court workshops in Istanbul for specific materials such as silks, carpets, and tiles. The number of artists and craftsmen within this system ranged from 600-900 at its largest. Court designers who had their own workshop were called *nakkaşan*. They not only decorated manuscripts for the court but also supplied patterns to the other court workshops. In this way new design creations were disseminated to various materials in a short time, and this gave Ottoman decorative arts a homogeneous look despite the variety of materials and production centers. The court workshops were usually equipped for relatively small-scale elite production and when the court needed large scale productions such as the tiles of large mosques, they reverted to commercial production by paying outside workshops directly. Carpets in Uşak and ceramics in Iznik were produced in this manner. The artists in these workshops were not salaried court artists but there was a strong relationship between these workshops and the court to maintain high standards. These outside craftsmen belonged to guilds with a religious structure where crafts and trades were learned through apprentice, assistant master and master training. The masters were approved by the sultans' certificate. The state generally supported the old masters holding this certificate. There was also close cooperation between the state and the guilds, and the state determined the quality of the goods under special regulations.

In Islamic art names and careers of artists are usually either unknown or difficult to assign to specific artworks. In the case of Ottoman art, we have enough documentary evidence to identify the names of a number of court artists and their creations. In certain cases we even know how much they were paid and sometimes how long they were hired by the court. Such evidence is amply recorded from the 16th century onwards, though not regularly, in the court records now preserved in the archive of the Topkapı Palace where the Ottoman sultans resided.

Outline of the book

This book is organized chronologically from 1299 to 1922 and the chapters are divided roughly according to the major styles in Ottoman decorative arts. There are more chapters reserved for the 15th and the 16th centuries as compared to those before and after. Each chapter is divided into three parts: Historical setting, Architectural activity and Decorative arts. 'Historical setting' aims at outlining the major political and social events of the period with an emphasis on the sultan. 'Architectural activity' provides information on the major buildings mostly sponsored by the Ottoman sultan and his entourage. The 'Decorative arts' section starts with a general outline of the period and then focuses on specific art works in different media. Due to the scale of the book only a selective group of objects and media are discussed for each period. For example, carpets are referred to in the chapters on the 16th century but not for the 17th. Special emphasis has been placed on selecting objects from collections in Turkey in the discussions.

The bibliography includes sources I used in various languages in the preparation of this book. The reader can select the appropriate ones for further reading as well.

Overall the book attempts to present scholarly research in a manner that would appeal to a wider audience of readers interested in the arts of the Ottomans or more generally arts from the Islamic past of present day Turkey. Ottoman decorative arts produced from the 14th to the early 20th century are explained concisely and illustrated with numerous colored images.

Terms

The following section explains some of the terms that are frequently used in the text but may be unfamiliar or confusing to the modern reader. A brief explanation of the term and its use in the Ottoman context is preferred over a technical explanation. More specific terms are explained in the text. Turkish words are written in modern Turkish spellings (Turkish was written in Arabic alphabet in Ottoman times).

Anatolia is a geographic term to indicate a large region of present day Turkey that lies outside the European continent.

Sultan is the ruler. All Ottoman sultans come from the same dynastic line that was established by Osman (1258?-1326?). The word Ottoman descended from Osman (or Otman in Turkish).

Mosque complex (*Külliye*) is a group of buildings that is centered on a mosque, the prayer hall for Muslims. These buildings usually included a school (*medrese*), bath (*hamam*), public soup kitchen (*imaret*), and a tomb.

Mihrab is the direction of Mecca usually emphasized as a large niche in the mosque.

Minaret is the tall and slender tower(s) connected to the mosque. Announcement for prayers are made five times a day from minaret.

Manuscripts: Ottoman manuscripts were written in Arabic alphabet although the language may have been Turkish, Persian or Arabic. The Arabic alphabet is written from right to left, thus the Ottoman manuscripts open from left to right. Each folio has a front (a) and back (b) side. Bindings of manuscripts were usually in leather, and had a separate section called the flap to envelop and protect the book.

Decorated Manuscripts: Although this term is not much used in scholarship it is helpful to refer to manuscripts with illuminations and illustrations as a whole. In European Art illuminated manuscripts refer to manuscripts with both figural and non-figural decoration. Unlike European art, strictly non-figural book decorations were produced in Islamic art, especially for Korans. These are studied as illuminated manuscripts. Illustrated manuscripts on the other hand include figural paintings and illuminations. Thus the European term 'illuminated manuscripts' blurs the significant difference between illuminated and illustrated manuscripts in Islamic art. For this reason decorated manuscripts are used instead in this book.

Calligraphy (*hat*) always held an important status in Islamic art due to the respect for the word of God embodied in the Koran. Like Arabic and Persian languages, Turkish was written in the Arabic alphabet by the Ottomans. The Arabic alphabet evolved through the centuries from an angular type of script to a rounded and cursive one. Famous calligraphers brought innovations which were followed for many centuries afterward. To the uneducated eye who is not accustomed to the rules of the Arabic alphabet, Islamic calligraphy can be appreciated for its flow and esthetic qualities. Seeing the innovations of famous calligraphers on the other hand requires more than a basic knowledge in Arabic script since copying held the utmost importance for the students of calligraphy. Calligraphers started practicing their arts by copying their masters. Thus following a master fully ensured the license from the master to the student necessary to practice this art independently. Only when calligraphers reached a certain maturity in their arts, and usually in age too, they were able to impose some changes to the established norms, if they were skilled enough to do so. Thus a calligrapher who was working in the 18th century might have been following a calligrapher who lived many centuries before him. This tradition of precise imitation of styles though important becomes an impediment in deciphering the hands of individual calligraphers unless we have reliable signed works. The word reliable is used here since some works are attributed to a certain famous calligrapher and are noted as such by later calligraphers. Thus the entirety of the work with its decoration (if there is any) is usually the key to the originality of the work by a certain calligrapher.

Illumination (*tezhib*) is a form of non-figural book decoration that included floral or geometric motifs. Copies of the Koran, which were never illustrated due to Islam's prohibition of figural decoration in religious contexts, were illuminated with floral and geometric designs in order to decorate them. Manuscripts of different topics often followed similar decorative styles as well. Usually the beginning and the end of manuscripts or the titles throughout the text were illuminated. These designs in time also changed in style and by detecting variations in motifs and the general layout on page one can have sufficient clues for the date of the illumination. Signed works by illuminators are of course key to the assignment of specific styles to certain illuminators and periods in the first place. Historical documents can sometimes give important information about certain artists and when combined with their signed works art historians can attribute more works to a specific illuminator. Sometimes as we shall see in the Ottoman case illuminators can also be calligraphers, binders and illustrators.

Illustrations, or miniatures as they are commonly known, are figural paintings that usually illustrate the written text in the manuscript or a theme that is described in the text. Despite the prohibition on figural painting in religious contexts illustrated manuscripts were produced in secular contexts as early as the 10th century in Islamic lands. Islamic rulers were ardent readers or owners of such books. The topics of illustrated manuscripts ranged from science to literary works. Iran and Central Asia under the patronage of Islamic rulers especially in the 14th and 15th centuries produced some of the most exquisite examples of illustrated and illuminated manuscripts. Ottoman sultans looked up to their Persian predecessors and contemporaries and tried to emulate their success in patronage of illustrated manuscripts. In this book we shall look at various works of Ottoman painters who collaborated with calligraphers and illuminators to create illustrated manuscripts usually sponsored by the Ottoman sultans, princes or important statesmen to read and take enjoyment in their illustrations. Some of the most distinguished Ottoman examples were Ottoman illustrated histories.

Works on paper: Ottoman artists did not always produce manuscripts. They also produced single drawings, portraits, paintings or calligraphic works.

Albums are collections of drawings, miniatures, and calligraphic samples from various time periods brought together to form a book. Some of the Ottoman works are now preserved in such albums and tell us much about the working techniques of certain artists.

Ceramics and tiles which were produced from clay with various inclusions to make them durable and glossy were made in Islamic lands from very early on. Either as vessels (ceramics) or as flat revetments (tiles) craftsmen made certain shapes, glazed them and fired them in kilns under high temperatures. Over time various techniques were created to achieve certain affects. Although other techniques will be discussed in this book, generally underglaze refers to the technique where surfaces were painted before they were glazed and fired in the kiln. Overglaze refers to the technique where some touch-ups were made after the initial firing and then a second firing under low temperatures was applied to affix the second layer. The Ottoman ceramic and tile industry produced one of the most sought after examples of this art form generally known as Iznik where they were made.

Chapter 2

Early trends: 1299-1451

Historical setting

The Ottoman dynasty which was established by Osman (reigned 1299?-1324) in the early 14th century in the northwestern part of present day Turkey had several other Turkish speaking Muslim principalities as well as the Byzantine Empire as its neighbors. The Byzantine Empire, or as it was known the Eastern Roman Empire, had reigned since the 3rd century but its territories in Anatolia were considerably smaller in the 12th-13th centuries due to the expansion of the Seljuk Turks who initially reigned in Iran. As the Seljuks slowly lost their power in the 13th century, small Turkish principalities asserted their powers in Anatolia. The Ottomans were only one of these and did not seem to have a higher status compared to the others. However, their proximity to the Byzantine Empire gave them an opportunity to expand their territories westward at the latter's expense. Early in the 14th century Osman's son Orhan (1324?-1362) managed to take control of important Byzantine cities and even crossed the Dardanelles. This westward expansion continued in the Balkans throughout the 14th century during the reign of Murad I (1362-1389) and Bulgaria and Serbia became tax-paying vassals of the Ottomans. In Anatolia several Turkish principalities also came under the control of the Ottomans. By the end of the 14th century, after the consecutive reigns of the first four Ottoman sultans, Osman, Orhan, Murad I and Bayezid I (1389-1402), a centralized Ottoman state stretching from the Danube to the Euphrates was created.

In the early 15th century Timur (Tamerlane) who created a powerful empire stretching from Central Asia to Iraq challenged the Ottoman sultan Bayezid I at the famous battle of Ankara. The Ottoman army lost the battle and sultan Bayezid was held captive at the hands of Timur and died. Under Timur's protection former principalities in Anatolia were reestablished and the remaining Ottoman territory was divided among Bayezid's sons, all of whom accepted Timur's sovereignty. This partition caused a decade-long power struggle among Bayezid's sons. During this period the rulers of Byzantium, Serbia, Walachia, and Albania regained some of their lands as well. In the end, the youngest son of Bayezid, Çelebi Mehmed (reigned as Mehmed I), was able to restore the unity of the Ottoman state under his personal sovereignty in 1413. He spent his time mostly to regain control of the former Ottoman territories in Anatolia while mainly keeping peaceful relations with the Christian rulers in the west. By the end of his reign he had not fully succeeded in restoring all the territorics his father Bayezid controlled before 1402. When Mehmed died in a riding accident in 1421 his oldest son Murad (II), aged only 17, became the sultan. He spent his early years trying to control the Ottoman power against other Ottoman contenders. After securing his right to the Ottoman throne he spent several years battling Anatolian principalities and the Byzantines after which he tried to maintain peaceful relations, and the Balkan powers at least for sometime. The war with the Venetians from 1423 to 1430 did not result in much gain for the Ottomans due to the lack of a powerful navy. But Murad II's advances in the 1430's in the Balkans opened up a new path for the Ottomans in Hungary and Serbia. Murad II left the throne to his young son Mehmed's control in 1444, but the dangerous advances of the Hungarian and Serbian rulers against the Ottomans forced Murad II to resume control from his son. The Ottoman army's successful battles in Varna (Bulgaria) in 1444 and Kosovo (former Yugoslavia) in 1448 definitively made the Balkans an Ottoman territory.

Among the first five sultans of the Ottomans, Orhan was the first to organize the administrative, military, and judiciary aspects of the Ottoman system. During Murad's reign janissaries (*yeniçeri*) were established as part of the Ottoman military system, and consisted of war captives who were trained to be Ottoman soldiers. Later Christian boys from the Balkans were also conscripted and trained as part of the janissary system. Bayezid I (1389-1402) was the first sultan who could read and write. Murad II is best known for his patronage of arts and artists. He was the first Ottoman sultan to compose poetry. His gathering of poets and scholars, even when he was a prince and governor in Amasya, was noted by Ottoman historians.

Architectural activity

During the 14th century Iznik, Bursa and Edirne served as the Ottoman capitals and new buildings such as forts, mosques, tombs, and *medreses* (schools) began to be erected. Existing buildings continued to be used sometimes with alterations for changing needs or functions. For example, the former Byzantine monastery in the Bursa fortress was converted into a *medrese* and the church of Hagia Sophia in Iznik was converted into a mosque. Orhan also built a group of buildings including a mosque, *medrese*, bath and closed market hall (*bezesten*) in Bursa. During the reigns of Murad I (1360-89) and Bayezid I (1389-1402), larger and more pretentious buildings with a large decorative program were erected. The Green Mosque at Iznik dated to 1378-1391 and built by the grand vizier Hayreddin Pasha had a large domed square plan, which became a standard for mosques in Ottoman architecture. Other plans were also used in mosque architecture such as the large Bursa mosque built on multiple piers (1395-1400) or the inverted T-shaped mosque in the complex of Bayezid in Bursa (1389-1402). *Medreses*, baths, tombs, and commercial buildings of this era can be seen primarily in Bursa and Iznik. A fort was built (the still standing Anadolu Hisarı) outside of Constantinople by Bayezid.

During the early 15th century Amasya, which is located in northern central Anatolia served Mehmed I as a center. Later when he consolidated Ottoman power in his hands, previous Ottoman centers in western Anatolia, Bursa and Edirne, respectively, once again became the Ottoman capitals and building activity continued, especially in Bursa. During Mehmed's reign the Green Mosque complex built in Bursa between 1419 and 1424 had the most embellished group of buildings. Its mosque, tomb, medrese, bath and public kitchen still survive. During the reign of Murad II, Edirne became the Ottoman capital and large-scale building activity took place in that city consisting of mosques, *medreses*, baths and a Sufi dervish lodge (*Mevlevihane*). Murad II's large mosque in Edirne, 'Mosque with a three balconied minaret' (*Üç Şerefeli Cami*) was built by an unknown architect but architecturally the building opened up a new phase of Ottoman architecture with its increasing dominance of a single dome as the central space and the arcaded courtyard which became an inseparable part of Ottoman mosques. Murad II also built a palace and a bridge (Uzunköprü) in Edirne and another palace in Manisa.

Decorative arts

Ottoman decorative arts from the 14th century are primarily limited to architectural decoration while those from the first half of the 15th century can be followed in a variety of materials: architectural decoration, decorated manuscripts, ceramics and carpets. Architectural decoration and decorated manuscripts show close ties with eastern Islamic centers, especially those in Iran and Central Asia under Timurid control. The similarity is partially due to the migration of artists, often involuntarily, during the havoc caused by the Timurid invasions, and partially to the dissemination of Timurid court habits to other Islamic courts. The ceramics and carpets on the other hand display local traditions of Islamic Anatolia.

Architectural decoration

The surviving specimens of architectural decoration show that the interiors of Ottoman buildings were painted with floral decorations on plaster or wood. This brushwork technique known as *kalemişi* in Turkish was mainly reserved for the upper sections of the buildings and was meant to accentuate or harmonize with the architectural forms, functions and styles of the buildings. An early and rare example can be seen around the large arched windows of the Kırgızlar tomb in Iznik, dated to the mid 14th century (Fig.2 Iznik Kırgızlar Tomb brushwork decoration). The scroll design seen on the decoration is known

Fig.2 Iznik Kırgızlar Tomb brushwork decoration

as 'arabesque' (*Rumi* in Turkish) and includes large split leafs. Paradoxically while the word in English reinforces the origin of the design to the early years of Islamic art, the Turkish word *Rumi* emphasizes the common use of this design in Anatolia, which was called Rum in reference to the Eastern Roman Empire. The scroll design is applied on plaster with red, black and orange colors on a plain background. Such floral designs were widely used in Anatolia before and contemporary to the Ottomans, and had deep roots in Islamic art very early onwards.

Colored and molded glazed tiles were used on the minarets of the newly built mosques in the 14th century. The minaret of the Green Mosque in Iznik built in 1378 displays geometric decoration made with molded and colored tiles of turquoise, cobalt blue, dark purple and black. The large geometric decoration on the minaret would attract the eye even from a distance. Creating geometric designs with molded and colored tiles was a known technique in Anatolia at the time and had been widely used in previous centuries by the Seljuks who ruled both in Iran and Anatolia. Thus craftsmen who were initially trained outside the Ottoman territories in this technique could have been easily assembled to work on specific Ottoman projects since the Ottoman state had enough revenues to offset such expenses.

Examples of tile work on the interior of Ottoman buildings are found in the 15th century. The famed Green Mosque (Yeşil Cami in Turkish), a medrese and tomb complex named after its turquoise tiles was built in Bursa by the fifth Ottoman sultan Mehmed I and completed by his son Murad II (Fig.3 Bursa Green Mosque). As in many other Ottoman buildings of this era these were decorated with tiles on the interior. But exceptionally, instead of being decorated with stone or marble decoration on its exterior, which was standard for Ottoman architecture, the tomb of the Green Mosque complex was also tiled on its exterior walls. This exception is clearly linked to a group of migrating artists: The tiles used on the *mihrab* niche display a calligraphic inscription and include the names of craftsmen from Tabriz. Tabriz, which is a western Iranian city, was under the control of the Turcoman dynasties and had a long tradition of tile and ceramic production in the 14th and 15th centuries. Inscriptions written in other parts of the building mention the name of another tile maker, Muhammed el-Mecnun, possibly of Iranian origin, as well as the local master artist who was in charge of the entire decoration, Ali ibn Ilyas, known as Nakkaş Ali of Bursa. Later Ottoman historians mention that this local artist had been taken to Samarkand when Timur invaded Anatolia. There he received his artistic training and brought eastern modes of decoration on his return when the Ottomans reasserted their power in Bursa. He also brought craftsmen from Tabriz and put them to work on the large Green Mosque project, generously sponsored by the Ottoman sultan, Mehmed I. The Ottoman vizier Hacı İvaz Pasha, who is recorded in the foundation inscription of the mosque as the supervisor of its construction, is also mentioned by later Ottoman historians to have invited foreign skilled artists to the Ottoman court.

Fig.3 Bursa Green Mosque

Nakkaş Ali was in charge of coordinating the decorative program of the Green Mosque which included tile work, wall paintings, woodwork and stone carving. He was able to create a harmony between the different elements of the design of the entire complex. Large areas of the interior walls, especially in the mosque and tomb, are covered with tiles made in several techniques (*cuerda seca*, monochrome glazed, and underglaze painted) (Fig.4 Bursa Green Mosque tiles). By combining different techniques, many more colors and intricate designs could be applied simultaneously on the tiled wall surfaces. In the *cuerda seca* technique, which is named after the Spanish term dry cord, a greasy substance is applied between different colors during firing in the kiln. This substance stops the colors from running into each other while it burns off and a large range of colors are achieved in various forms. This technique was known at Timurid Samarkand in the 14th century and was used in combination with other tiling techniques in the 15th century. It is thus possible that the Tabrizi artists were originally taken by Timur to Samarkand where they learned this new technique and combined it with their local knowledge of cut mosaics. The Green Mosque complex in Bursa is especially a showcase for the *cuerda seca* tiles and its combined use with other tiling techniques as in Timurid buildings in Samarkand. The *mihrab*,

Fig.4 Bursa Green Mosque tiles

Fig.5 Bursa Green Complex, Tomb of Mehmed I

walls of the tomb and the sarcophagi in the tomb, which belong to Mehmed I and his sons, are decorated with *cuerda seca* tiles (Fig.5 Bursa Green Complex, Tomb of Mehmed I). The designs on the walls have parallels in Timurid bindings. The sarcophagus of Mehmed I flawlessly depicts large calligraphic bands in bright yellow over a dark blue ground in this technique. Stylized floral designs in arched shapes complement the calligraphic band in the lower part of the sarcophagus. Colors of pistachio green, blue, brown, white, and purple are seen in the details of the design.

The rich tile decoration, which displayed new colors, was applied in Anatolia for the first time in this building. The exterior decoration of the tomb with tiles was also an eastern feature which was not typical for the Ottomans. Unfortunately the original ones on the tomb have been mostly lost and what we see today is mainly composed of modern tiles. It is suggested that Tabrizi craftsmen set up temporary workshops to work on this and other Ottoman buildings in the 15th century, rather then producing them in one center and sending them out from there.

Although the building may have been exceptional in its tile decoration, it is suggested to foreshadow a uniquely Ottoman taste in its general principals of architectural decoration: interiors decorated with tiles, marble and brushwork (*kalemişi*) on plaster. The tile decoration was used in the lower sections of the walls, and reached a greater height only around the windows and *mihrab* niche. The areas above the tiles were plastered and brushwork decorations were painted in specific areas around architectural elements as accents, although not much has survived from the original state. This program of interior decoration, namely to use color in terms of tiles and brushwork on plaster to emphasize architectural elements, becomes a common feature of classical Ottoman architecture in the 16th century.

A later building also in Bursa shows the use of more common monochrome glazed tiles. Bursa Muradiye Mosque built in 1425 by Murad II is decorated with tiles forming large geometric compositions in the lower section of its interiors. As in Bursa Green Mosque some of them were stamped with gold leaf to form a second layer of floral decorations in a circular pattern (similar to the hexagonal tiles in fig.4). This gilded surface was applied by a second firing on the already glazed tiles at low temperatures in the kiln and thus rubbed off relatively quickly. Today usually only traces of these gilded surfaces can be seen on the dark blue glazed tiles in several Ottoman buildings from the 15th century.

The decoration of another mosque with the same name 'Muradiye' in Edirne also built by Murad II reinforces the eastern connections of the Ottoman decorative repertoire during this early period. Edirne Muradiye Mosque was built in 1426-27 as part of a building complex but today only the mosque survives. It displays an extraordinary selection of tiles in its prayer hall. The *mihrab* is covered with *cuerda seca* tiles as in Bursa Green Mosque. In addition large surfaces from the ground up to the eye level on the sidewalls are faced with blue and white hexagonal tiles with turquoise triangular tiles in between (Fig.6 Edirne Muradiye Mosque tiles).The hexagonal tiles display numerous compositions of central floral designs in blue on a white ground, and less frequently white on a bluc ground. These patterns owe a lot in inspiration to Chinese blue and white ceramics, especially in their use of peony and lotus flowers. The transmission from the Chinese to the Ottomans seems however indirect: The Timurids imported high quality porcelain-like blue and white ceramics from China in high quantities in the early 15th century. These created a taste for applying blue and white tiles to the exterior and interior walls of Timurid buildings in Central Asia, especially in Samarkand until the mid-15th century. The artists who knew the Timurid applications must have brought this taste to the Ottoman world as well. In fact their use simultaneously with the *cuerda seca* tiles on the same building and the technical analysis of the tiles show that the project was entirely carried out by the 'Tabrizi artists' who also worked on the Green Mosque in Bursa.

Fig.6 Edirne Muradiye Mosque tiles

Fig.7 Edirne Muradiye Mosque brushwork decoration

The rarely surviving painted work on plaster in the same building adds another layer to our understanding of decorative arts in the early Ottoman era. As was common in previous Ottoman buildings, the painted work was applied on plaster above the tiled walls (Fig.7 Edirne Muradiye Mosque brushwork decoration). Mainly elongated floral compositions set in vases, collar designs in the shape of clouds, and circular calligraphic panels decorated the walls. Such patterns are commonly found initially in Timurid and later in Ottoman book decorations of the 15th century. The overall design is suggested to reflect a landscape filled with flowers and blossoming trees. Although the actual buildings do not survive, this type of landscape design is commonly seen on the interiors of royal buildings in Timurid miniatures and is thought to reflect a paradise-like setting in accordance with Islamic thought.

Decorated Manuscripts

The first half of the 15th century saw the first production of Ottoman decorated manuscripts in Amasya, Bursa, and Edirne. These manuscripts were mainly copies of literary or poetic works by Turkish or Persian authors. Turkish was the native tongue and Persian was the literary language at the Ottoman court and literary circles. The Ottoman sultans were well versed in Persian. The manuscripts had a few pages decorated with floral and geometric designs called illuminations before and after the text, or sometimes throughout the text as titles. The manuscripts were bound in fine leather bindings that were also decorated. While some manuscript decorations show influences from the western Iranian courts in Shiraz, others reflect the Mamluk world of Syria and Egypt. Some bindings and illuminations in Ottoman manuscripts display a similarity to the tile work and painted decoration on contemporary architectural monuments in Bursa and Edirne. Thus we may propose that artists of each medium shared similar designs and probably worked closely at a court setting.

The first illustrated Ottoman manuscript now in Paris is dated to 1416, and is an early copy of a Turkish work, *Iskendername*, by Ahmedi. Ahmedi (d.1412) composed his work on the well known story of Alexander the Great in Islamic literature. The manuscript was copied in Amasya in 1416 during the reign of Mehmed I while his son prince Murad (II) was residing there as a governor. Thus it is likely that the manuscript was intended for this prince who enjoyed the company of poets in many of the gatherings he organized during his six years of government in this city. The manuscript was meant to have twenty-one miniatures but only three illustrations were painted directly on the paper and the others were created by cutting up earlier miniatures from Iran and pasting them in simple painted settings. Despite the unusual arrangement of the miniatures they were closely linked to the text. The three miniatures were made in a style reminiscent of Byzantine paintings. Thus perhaps a Christian artist worked on the decorations of the manuscript but was unable to create an Islamic style for the illustrations. Why he was hired to work on this manuscript in the first place is unknown but may well be related to the scarcity of artists in Amasya who could execute twenty miniatures in an Islamic style. Not only the figurative style of the artist but his floral decorative frames around the miniatures can be seen on some 15th century Armenian manuscripts from Eastern Anatolia. Interestingly Armenian illumination of this period was deeply influenced by Islamic styles of the surrounding areas. Thus a reciprocal decorative vocabulary was used in both realms. The same type of floral decorations, namely sprouting flowers can be easily compared to the brushwork decorations in Edirne Muradiye Mosque dated circa 1430 (see fig. 7). The adherence to Timurid designs in various media and distant geographies just shows how widespread this eastern Islamic taste was through the migration of artists and styles in the 15th century.

Beyond the somewhat unusual floral decorations of the Ahmedi *Iskendername*, the first truly illuminated Ottoman manuscript in the Islamic sense was a manuscript dedicated to Murad II. This manuscript *Mekasid al-Alhan*, (Fig.8 *Mekasid al-Alhan,* Topkapı Palace Museum R. 1726 1b-2a) was a copy of a contemporary Persian text on musical theory. The author Abd al-Kadir al-Maraghi (d. 1435) was the greatest composer-performer of his day and wrote about musical instruments as well as rhythmic cycles and modal systems in music. The manuscript opens with two facing illuminated pages. The left one contains a dedication to the treasury of Murad II. Each page is designed differently. The first page (on the right since the book opens to the right) has a round medallion with an arabesque scroll design at its center and the facing page has an ogival (pointed oval) central medallion that contains the gold dedicatory inscription. On both pages decorations in the corners extend beyond the corners thereby producing elaborate designs filled with arabesque scrolls. The area around the central medallion is reduced to narrow irregularly shaped bands filled with leaf sprays. The details of this design, especially the cloud-shaped collar designs in the four corners and the central medallion, are close to brushwork decorations of Edirne Muradiye Mosque (compare fig. 7). The cloud-shaped collar motif, which was initially used on Timurid costumes, was later adopted for bindings or illuminations of books. Some of the artists working for the Ottoman court may have initially come from the Timurid world or local artists may have learned such designs from the works of their Timurid colleagues. The manuscript also has an exquisite leather binding (Fig. 9 *Mekasid al-Alhan,* Topkapı Palace Museum R. 1726 binding) in which front and back covers bear different designs that echo the differences between the two illuminated pages. The oval medallion on the front cover is decorated with an arabesque design similar to the

Fig.8 Mekasid al-Alhan, Topkapı Palace Museum R. 1726 1b-2a

Fig. 9 Mekasid al-Alhan, Topkapı Palace Museum R. 1726 binding

one on the illumination. The wide borders are designed with a geometric braid decoration. The interiors of the covers and the flap are made of darker colored leather as it was common in Ottoman bindings of the 15th century. They are decorated with a filigree (cut out) geometric design. In the filigree technique the empty parts of the leather decoration were cut out allowing the colored cloth or paper underneath to be seen.

In addition to the Timurid influences on Ottoman manuscript decoration we also see Mamluk influences, especially on Ottoman Koran copies. The Mamluks who ruled in Syria and Egypt were famous for their large exquisitely illuminated Korans.

Ceramics

Iznik which became the first Ottoman capital in 1331 was a center of ceramic production in the 14th and 15th centuries. Modern excavations conducted in this town show that the so-called Miletus ware of these centuries (named after the finds in this classical site in western Turkey) was in fact produced in Iznik. These ceramics were made of a red clay and were painted with a dark tone of blue with additions of purple, green or black over a white material called slip and under a transparent glaze. The slip technique which produced a white ground despite the red clay underneath tried to imitate the expensive and imported blue and white Chinese porcelains fashionable at various Islamic courts in the 15th century. These early Iznik wares were widely used in rural and urban areas. They were decorated with simple designs, and the workmanship does not show very high standards of execution. However, the ceramic production in this city saw major developments in the late 15th and 16th centuries, which were probably laid on the foundations of this early ceramic production.

Carpets

Surviving carpets clearly show that carpets were produced in Anatolia at least from the 12th-13th centuries onwards. Written documents indicate that the Ottomans also played a great role in the carpet trade between Europe and Anatolia in the 15th century. Ottoman cities of Bursa and Iznik are noted to be centers of carpet production in the early 15th century, which is the date of the earliest surviving Ottoman carpets. Their decoration consists of two main frames in the field and smaller repeating geometrical motifs on the border. The main frames were either filled with geometrical animal figures of birds, dragons and deer or large geometric diamond motifs. These motifs, especially the stylized animal figures, on these carpets do not display any connections to Ottoman wall paintings, tiles or book illuminations of the period, but rather owe a great deal to the nomadic traditions of Anatolia which have deep roots in pre-Islamic Central Asia.

Chapter 3

Formation of Ottoman court styles: 1451-1512

Historical setting

When Mehmed II came to power in 1451 he was only 21 years old and his father had already left the throne to Mehmed's control during his lifetime between 1444 and 1446. Although he was still considered young and inexperienced by his Christian and Muslim enemies, Mehmed's conquest of Constantinople on 29 May 1453 gave him the title 'the conqueror' (Fatih in Turkish) and great prestige in Europe and the Islamic world. In the eyes of the Islamic world he succeeded where Arab armies of the 8th century had failed. In Europe he was seen as the heir to the Byzantine Empire. After this conquest, Mehmed made the Byzantine city Constantinople his center and publicized his aim to control both the Christian dominated lands in the Balkans, Crimea, and Italy, and the Muslim territories of Anatolia and the East.

In accordance with his newly assumed role, Mehmed made a series of campaigns in the Balkans in the first fourteen years after his conquest of Constantinople in order to maintain control over these areas and to eliminate the local dynasties. He also took full control of the Dardanelles and decreased the dominance of Venetian maritime power in Istanbul. After Bosnia came under Ottoman control Venice felt the threat and started a long war against the Ottomans. After peace talks during the years 1468-73, the Venetian war ended in 1479 with a peace treaty that forced the Venetians to pay a large annual tribute to the Ottomans. In the east Mehmed annexed the

Anatolian Karamanid principality in 1468 and won a decisive victory in 1473 against the Turcoman Akkoyunlu dynasty. This dynasty was also ruled by Turkish speaking rulers in eastern Anatolia and western Iran. By the end of Mehmed's reign, the territorial extent of the Ottoman state had doubled and eighteen new provinces had been annexed.

Mehmed II is remembered not only as a great statesman but also as a learned man of his age. The books in his library show that he was interested in history, geography, philosophy, military science, medicine, and religion of both the Islamic and the Christian traditions written in Turkish, Persian, Arabic, Greek, and Latin. He had a strong interest in Ancient history (Hesiod, Homer, Ptolemy, Arrian, Diogenes Laertius, and Xenephon) and his doctors trained in Greek and Latin read him passages from these books everyday. He was especially interested in the life of Alexander the Great to whom Mehmed was compared by contemporary historians. He also had histories of his own reign written in Turkish, Persian, and Greek. He gathered various scholars of his age from Italy and Islamic lands in his court and supported artists and poets. He is the first Ottoman sultan to have a collection of poems (*divan*). He issued the first Ottoman law code as well as the first Ottoman golden coin. Among Ottoman sultans Mehmed II was the first sultan to be buried in Istanbul.

Bayezid II, who had spent 27 years as a prince and governor in Amasya ascended the throne in 1481 at the age of 34. Immediately he had a power conflict with his brother Cem, the governor of Karaman. In June of the same year Bayezid won a battle against Cem's army with the support of the janissaries. Cem escaped to Egypt and tried to attack Bayezid with a new army that he had been given by the Mamluk sultan, Kaitbay. Once again Bayezid defeated Cem who then took refuge at Rhodes with the Knights of St. John. Bayezid, fearing that a union of Western states would use Cem against him, paid large sums of money (45.000 ducats yearly) to the Knights to imprison Cem first in France and later in Naples. Cem stayed under their control until his death in February 1495, having never been able to return to Ottoman territory. Bayezid's successful campaign in Moldavia in 1484 gave him considerable prestige and power. In 1495, the Ottomans made a truce with the Hungarians and in 1499 with the Poles. During 1499-1502 the Ottomans waged another war against the Venetians. The Ottoman fleet challenged Venice on the open sea and as a result Lepanto (in present day Greece) fell to the Ottomans in 1499. In 1502, a peace agreement made with Venice ratified important gains for the Ottomans on the Adriatic shore and in the Morea.

From 1503 to 1512, Bayezid faced problems in the East. A Shiite order named Safaviyya (one of two Islamic sects, the Ottomans adhered to the Sunni sect) took control of the Akkoyunlu dominions. Its influence over the Turcoman tribes in the eastern regions of the Ottoman lands posed a threat to Ottoman control over the regions along the Taurus frontier and a risk of further division in Anatolia. Bayezid instigated harsh measures. He deported Shiite groups to Morea and used military force against the army of Ismail, the Akkoyunlu ruler. During the same time Bayezid's sons Selim and Ahmed began a violent struggle over the Ottoman throne during their father's lifetime. In the end Bayezid accepted to abdicate the throne in favor of Selim but died soon after on May 1512 en route to his place of retirement.

Bayezid II, who was educated in the Edirne and Amasya palaces, was very interested in poetry and like his father composed poetry himself. He was also interested in history, Islamic philosophy, astrology, cosmography, and mechanics. Ottoman history writing became important during his reign. He generously supported poets, historians, and artists. He had a close relationship with Sufi brotherhoods and was referred to as Sofu (Sufi) and Veli (friend of God) by his contemporaries. He was interested in calligraphy and overall he was more traditional and pious compared to his father. There was also more cultural activity due to peaceful and stable times compared to his father's reign.

Architectural activity

Mehmed II's reign was marked by the conquest of Constantinople in 1453. Leading to this event he built a new fort outside the city (Rumeli Hisarı) in a very short time. When the city was conquered Mehmed himself tried as much as he could to prevent the wholesale destruction of the city in the hands of the Ottoman army. He learned about the city's past from Greek sources and tried to bring the glory of the city's past, which had been lost in the declining years of Byzantine rule, to its new role as the Ottoman capital known to the Turks as Istanbul. Soon after its conquest it became an important center for Ottoman arts and architecture. Damaged city walls were rebuilt. Several Byzantine buildings were converted to perform new functions to satisfy the needs of the Ottoman court and the Muslim populations that moved there. For example the famed church of the city, Hagia Sophia, was converted into a mosque. The changes in the building were not initially major and its mosaics remained uncovered for a long time. Hagia Sophia also became the first school (*medrese*) in the city.

New buildings were also quickly erected. A large covered trade center which is the core of the present day 'Covered Bazaar' of Istanbul was begun in 1455. A palace was built in the center of the city. Later another one, the New Palace (Saray-ı Cedid), the present day Topkapı Palace was built in the 1460's on the outer edge of the historical peninsula, the former acropolis. Compared to the first palace, the elevation of the chosen ground for the new palace made it prominently visible to those who approached the city from the sea. This palace became the permanent residence of the Ottoman sultans from Mehmed's time until the 19th century (since the 19th century it came to be called the Topkapı Palace after the nearby cannon -gate (top-kapı) and was turned into a museum in 1924). The new palace comprised of several buildings. It was surrounded with walls and European styled towers. It included a main gateway, a secondary gateway, private living quarters, a council hall of justice, treasury, a small mosque, bath, and kitchens. The Byzantine church Hagia Eirene was incorporated into the outer court of the palace and later garden pavilions were also added by Mehmed. Although garden pavilions in Ottoman and European styles have perished, the Persianate Tiled Kiosk (Çinili Köşk) survives (it can be visited as part of the Istanbul Archaeological Museum located adjacent to the Topkapı Palace Museum). The palace was built by architects from Ottoman lands as well as those from Arab, Persian, and possibly European lands. The 15th century Venetian painter Gentile Bellini was also invited for the decoration of the palace although none of his work has been physically documented.

Mehmed built a large mosque complex in his name (Fatih, Conqueror) that included religious, social, and commercial buildings in the city center. The mosque was built according to its inscription between 1463 and 1470, on the fourth hill of the city, which was previously occupied by the second largest church of the city. The mosque which had a large dome (it was rebuilt after an earthquake in 1765) was a showcase of Ottoman architecture in the city at that time. It differed from the mosque types in Bursa and Edirne and opened a path for the types of large mosques of Istanbul, which still dominate the Istanbul skyline. The large complex included 16 *medreses* of higher learning, a hospital, a guesthouse, a public soup kitchen, a caravanserai, a bath, a primary school, and a library. With all of its buildings the Fatih complex surpassed all previous examples of Ottoman architecture and remained so for almost a century in Istanbul. Today only some of the original buildings survive. The complex eventually gave its name, Fatih, to the surrounding neighborhood.

Several other mosque complexes and mosques continued to be built by the sultan and his viziers. Large endowments were set for the maintenance of these buildings and services provided in them. By the end of Mehmed's reign, Istanbul was already transformed into an Islamic city with relevant institutions. The city's population included Muslims, Orthodox Greeks, Jews, Armenians, and Europeans. It also became the commercial center of the state. In the meantime architectural activity continued in other cities as well.

Major mosque complexes were built by Bayezid II in Amasya on the bank of the Yeşilırmak river (1486), in Edirne near the Tunca river bank (1484-87), and in Istanbul in the city center (1501-1506). The Bayezid complex in Istanbul also gave its name to the neighborhood, as did his father's complex in Fatih. Bayezid's complexes in all three cities were quite large and included various buildings such as a hospital, medical school, fountain, guesthouse, bathhouse, kitchens, and stores, and thus served as social–religious centers. The complexes in Edirne and possibly in Istanbul were built by architect Hayreddin of whom we know very little. The complex in Istanbul was built in five years according to its foundation inscription. With a smaller dome the Bayezid mosque establishes a variation on the plan of the Fatih mosque. Unlike the Fatih mosque it has survived in its original state. The first dervish lodge (*mevlevihane*) was built in Istanbul by Bayezid as well. His viziers and court officials also contributed to building activity throughout the empire.

Decorative arts

The second half of the 15th century opens a new chapter in Ottoman decorative arts as the Ottomans begin to pursue an imperial worldview. Ottoman decorative arts benefited both from the western and eastern expansion of the Ottoman territories during the second half of the 15th century. We will see that the continuing influence of the eastern Islamic art of the Timurids made its way into a new Ottoman style that was created under the sponsorship of the court and disseminated into various materials. Decorated manuscripts, ceramics and carpets of this period best illustrate the impact of this new court style. Some European elements also made their way into Ottoman decorative arts during this period, especially on works on paper, illustrated manuscripts and ceramics. However, these influences did not find much of a chance to develop. Overall we can conclude that the second half of the 15th century set the standards for Ottoman arts that would continue to expand even further under court patronage in the following century.

Works on paper and decorated manuscripts

During the reigns of Mehmed II and Bayezid II the production of Ottoman decorated manuscripts reached unprecedented levels. The homogeneity of illumination and bindings in several manuscripts of the second half of the 15th century suggest that there was clearly a court studio in Istanbul as early as the 1460's to supply the increasing demand for decorated manuscripts by the court. This is the first time we can speak of an Ottoman court studio in history. The term *nakkaşhane* generally refers to this studio at least starting from the reign of Bayezid II. In the court studio not only were decorated manuscripts produced but also designs to be applied to other media. Although Ottoman documents mentioning a court studio have not survived for the period of Mehmed II, a few court records document the existence of a court studio during the reign of Bayezid II. A register of 1494-1511 lists a total of 22 designer-artists (*nakkaş*) who were paid by the court during this period. Some of them had come from Iran. We also learn from similar but later records that Hasan bin Abdülcelil, also known as Hasan Çelebi, who continued to be employed until 1536, was the head of the court studio during the last two years of Bayezid's reign (1510-12).

Although the artists working for the court may not have worked together in a modern studio-like place all the time, there is some evidence on the place of the court studio for the late 15th century. Court artists who produced luxury manuscripts and designs to be applied to other media are believed to have been assigned to some special and perhaps temporary quarters in the palace. There is also a document dated to 1527-8, which mentions the second floor of a converted church that was used for this purpose outside the walls of the Topkapı Palace. The lower level was used as a menagerie and the building was therefore called *Arslanhane*. Later visual and written sources indicate that a building adjacent to the *Arslanhane* was used as the court studio. It is possible that this building may also have been used for the same purpose in the 15th century. Since we know from later periods that artists did not always work together in a studio, the building may have been used to hold regular meetings by artists to go over the details of their assumed projects, rather then as their constant workplace.

A register of imperial gifts (*inam defteri*) from the reign of Bayezid records the names of artists (*nakkaş*), the works they presented to the sultan on specific occasions (mostly religious festivals), and the amount of money in cash or goods they received as their reward. In general, the value of what they received from the sultan was much higher than the gifts they presented. In fact, it is suggested that by using this system the court was able to pay small amounts to artists as salaries and to encourage them to produce important works to be presented to the sultan in order to receive additional compensation.

A new style that dominated the arts of the period is suggested to have been created by Baba Nakkaş, the first of a series of court artists who dominated the Ottoman decorative arts. Baba Nakkaş (which means master designer in Turkish), whose real name was Mehmed, was a Sufi sheikh, possibly of Central Asian origin. He is documented to have received a large land as a gift from the sultan, and considered to be an important artist working for the Ottoman court. An album containing material from the reign of Mehmed II includes various drawings for tiles, manuscript illuminations, ceramics, and textiles datable to around the 1460's and 1470's (Fig. 10 Album, Istanbul University Library, F. 1423, 28b-29a). Although these designs are generally inspired by Timurid models they differ in the details. The drawings of these new creations are attributed to Baba Nakkaş. This style, which combined arabesques with Chinese inspired flowers in compact circular patterns, was probably created under the direct patronage of Mehmed II.

Fig.10 Album, Istanbul University Library, F. 1423, 28b-29a

Illuminations and bindings of various manuscripts made under Mehmed's patronage clearly reflect this style. A specific type of 'oak leaf' shaped palmet has curling tips and thus gives a sense of three-dimensionality. Split leaves of the arabesques are depicted with large lobes and minute parallel hatching is visible in the leaves. As we shall see the Baba Nakkaş style not only appeared on decorated manuscripts but was disseminated to the decorative program of other arts of the period such as ceramics, metalwork, carpets, and woodwork. Obviously Baba Nakkaş was not the only artist working for the court who was influential in the dissemination of this style to other media. Unfortunately we do not know most of their names. Some artists who worked on the decorated manuscripts are better known.

The decorated manuscripts produced in this period still had a strong connection with the Iranian world. It was also a time period in which several illustrated manuscripts were produced for the first time and even more were decorated with only illuminations and bound with exquisite bindings. Both Mehmed II and Bayezid II were bibliophiles and several decorated manuscripts bear dedications to them. Not only Ottoman sultans but their sons and viziers were also sponsors of this production. Initially Amasya, Bursa, Edirne, and, after the 1460's, Istanbul, became the main cities where decorated manuscripts were produced for the Ottoman sultans, their sons, and viziers. They included a wide range of topics from religion to rhetoric, math to geography. The personal interests of the sultans obviously were reflected on the type of manuscripts produced for them.

An illuminated manuscript on medical science by Ibn-i Sina, which was dedicated to Mehmed II, has a double illuminated page that contains the dedication to Mehmed II (Fig.11 *Kanun fil tibb*, Nuruosmaniye Library, 3571, 1b-2a). The illuminations show clear similarities with the Baba Nakkaş style. The bindings

Fig.11 Kanun fil tibb, Nuruosmaniye Library, 3571, 1b-2a

of several decorated manuscripts from the reign of Mehmed II also bear close similarities to the Baba Nakkaş style.

Korans were made in large numbers during the reign of Bayezid. The reason for this shift is generally attributed to the preferences of Bayezid who was personally involved in religious orders and considered to have been far more conventionally pious than his father had been. Bayezid's active patronage of the calligrapher Şeyh (Sheikh) Hamdullah is well documented. When Bayezid was in Amasya as a governor, his patronage of this calligrapher had turned the city into a center for the study and practice of calligraphy. After Bayezid ascended to the throne in 1481 he brought Şeyh Hamdullah to Istanbul and provided him with special quarters in the palace. Several illuminated Korans copied by him (a total of 47) attest that Şeyh Hamdullah developed a new calligraphic style around 1485, which set the standard for over a hundred and fifty years in Ottoman calligraphy.

These Korans, some of which were dedicated to Bayezid II, were bound in fine leather bindings and had several fully illuminated pages at various points in the text. The execution of this illumination is very fine and valuable materials such as gold and lapis (that gives the blue color) were abundantly used. A Koran which was copied by Şeyh Hamdullah in 1496 exemplifies the high quality of calligraphy, illumination and binding in a court sponsored manuscript (Fig.12 Koran, Topkapı Palace Museum, EH. 72, 2b-3a). Şeyh Hamdullah calls himself 'scribe of the sultan' at the end of the manuscript where it is customary to put a date and the name of the scribe. The manuscript measures 18x26cm and is copied in the *naskh* script, which was favored most by Şeyh Hamdullah. The binding of the manuscript repeats the minute motifs of the illumination, and has a brown exterior and burgundy interior.

Fig.12 Koran, Topkapı Palace Museum, EH. 72, 2b-3a

The exterior decoration consists of a central oval medallion and four corner pieces. The interior also repeats the same general plan but with larger areas left blank and more abundant use of gold to contrast with the burgundy color.

The reigns of Mehmed and Bayezid saw the first blooming of illustrated Ottoman manuscripts. The styles of the miniatures owed a great deal to those in contemporary Iranian manuscripts especially of Shiraz. A few artists from Iranian centers of book production, such as Shiraz and Tabriz, are known to have arrived at the Ottoman court but there must have been a growing number of local artists as well. The Turkish *Iskendername* by Ahmedi was a popular topic and continued to be produced with miniatures during the reign of Mehmed II (See the previous chapter for the first Ottoman example dated to 1416). At least three illustrated copies of this text were produced during the reign of Mehmed. One with sixty-six high quality miniatures was most likely made for Mehmed II himself (now in Venice). Another one with forty miniatures (now in St. Petersburg) may have been produced under the patronage of Mehmed's vizier Mahmud Pasha. An undated manuscript of poetry by the famous 15th century Persian poet Katibi was also illustrated with two miniatures (Fig.13 *Külliyat-ı Katibi*, Topkapı Palace Museum, H. 989, 93a). One miniature which illustrates a poem about the pleasures of the tambourine (*def*) and reed flute (*ney*) shows the entertainment of a sultan surrounded by court officials some of whom wear the typical headgear of the Ottoman household officers in the palace. The long white felt headgear folded to the back was also worn by the janissaries. The sultan is entertained by drinks and music which includes

Fig.13 Külliyat-ı Katibi, Topkapı Palace Museum, H. 989, 93a

the sounds of the tambourine and the reed flute. The gilded tiles behind the sultan, male and female headgears, blue and white ceramics and golden vessels held by servants most likely represent the real entertainment, decoration and objects of the court of Mehmed II. It is this documentary aspect of the miniatures that became dominant in Ottoman illustrated manuscripts.

Mehmed II also had an interest in European portrait tradition. He asked several Italian rulers, namely the Medici, the lord of Rimini, the King of Naples, and the Venetian Doge, to send European artists to the Ottoman court. A few are known to have actually arrived at the Ottoman court. Constanzo da Ferrera of Naples (originally of Venice), who produced a medal with the bust portrait of Mehmed II, was possibly in Istanbul sometime in 1475-81. Sculptor Bartolomeo Bellona of Padua and Gentile Bellini of Venice also came to the Ottoman capital. Bellini, who probably stayed the longest between 1479 and 1481, is known to have painted frescoes on the walls of a pavilion of the sultan although none have been documented. Only one of Bellini's oil paintings of Mehmed II is preserved today (National Gallery in London). In this painting Bellini portrayed Mehmed as a middle aged man wearing a fur-trimmed caftan and large turban in the Ottoman fashion. The inscription on the painting refers to him as the 'Conqueror of the World'. Bellini also made medals of the Sultan in a similar pose with inscriptions referring to him as the sultan and the emperor. This is exactly how Mehmed II wanted his European peers to know him, the sultan of the Ottomans and heir to the Byzantine Empire.

The impact of Mehmed's interest in European painting and medals is found on Ottoman arts, such as paintings on paper and illustrated manuscripts. An artist called Nakkaş Sinan Bey is recorded by a 16th century Ottoman historian to have been trained by a Venetian artist, Mastori Pavli ('Master Pavli' remains to be unknown) who was visiting Istanbul during the reign of Mehmed II. Sinan Bey also had a student named Ahmed Şiblizade from Bursa. Two paintings on paper, which depict the Ottoman sultan Mehmed II, are attributed to these Ottoman artists. One shows more European features and is attributed to Sinan since he was directly trained by Italian masters. In this painting Mehmed is shown in profile as a bust portrait similar to the image on his medals. The other one (Fig. 14 Album, Topkapı Palace Museum, H. 2153, 10a) is attributed to Şiblizade Ahmed and depicts Mehmed sitting cross-legged, holding a handkerchief and smelling a rose, as it was common to depict Islamic rulers. Şiblizade Ahmed blends the eastern and western features to a higher degree than his teacher. In both paintings in addition to the traditional line drawing we see tonal rendering of the surfaces similar to the European convention of depicting the third dimension by the application of shadow and light.

Several miniatures in manuscripts made during the reign of Bayezid reflect more of these European elements. Despite the general view that Bayezid II was more pious than his father the numbers of illustrated manuscripts made during his time increased. While this may have been just an accident of the surviving record, the existence of European elements in many

Fig.14 Album, Topkapı Palace Museum, H. 2153, 10a

miniatures of Bayezid's reign show that his personal attitudes did not hinder the natural development of an interest in European painting styles at least among Ottoman painters.

During Bayezid's reign, the famous love story between the Persian King Khusraw (590-628) and the Armenian princess Shirin was illustrated. The story had become a literary classic after the one written by the Iranian poet Nizami and was previously illustrated in other Islamic courts of Iran and Central Asia. A Turkish version of the story was composed by Şeyhi in the first half of the 15th century but illustrated copies of it only survive from the reign of Bayezid (1481-1512). At least four copies of the Turkish version and two copies by the late 15th century Persian poet Hatifi were illustrated in the Ottoman realm. In many of the miniatures of these six copies and those of manuscripts on other literary topics, the use of shading to indicate the third dimension, the addition of architectural elements shown from a perspectival view, and atmospheric rendition of skies can be clearly seen.

An Ottoman miniature added to a Persian manuscript (dated to 1498) that must have come to the court of Bayezid shows some of these elements (Fig.15 *Khamsa* of Dihlavi, Topkapı Palace Museum, H. 799, 182a). In this miniature the Persian hero Bahram Gur is shown in the Red Pavilion with the Russian Princess as told in the story. Bahram Gur and the princess are seated in front of an octagonal pavilion that occupies the painting's middle ground. The buildings shown in the miniature have

Fig.15 Khamsa of Dihlavi, Topkapı Palace Museum, H. 799, 182a

similarities with examples depicted in Byzantine paintings that could have been visible on icons and wall paintings in churches in Istanbul. The shaded rendition of the roofs and walls and attempts at perspective on the buildings themselves are typical for the Ottoman miniatures of this period.

This trend which must have come to the Ottoman court at the very end of Mehmed II's reign did not last long. The artists experimented with these techniques during the reign of Bayezid and incorporated them into a more distinct style of Ottoman miniatures in the late 15th century. These elements gave Ottoman miniatures a certain character that separated them from their Islamic, especially Iranian counterparts. However once these elements became standard in the 16th century they lost their reference to their original European models. Overall under Bayezid's patronage Ottoman arts of the book achieved higher standards and the court studio continued to be the center of artistic excellence and creativity.

Architectural decoration

Surviving monuments built in the second half of the 15th century show that tile techniques and wall decorations in brushwork continued to follow eastern, Timurid fashions as in the first part of the 15th century.

Although Mehmed II's mosque in Istanbul does not retain its original state due to a major rebuilding after an earthquake in 1765, two surviving tile decorations of window arches from the courtyard of the mosque can be attributed to the original decoration of the building dated to 1463-70. It appears that here the artists who executed the Green Mosque complex in Bursa and the Muradiye Mosque in Edirne in the first half of the 15th century moved to this project and copied the motifs of their trademark *cuerda seca* tiles in the under glaze technique. This change in technique most likely was a way to decrease the time and labor necessary to execute the same amount of tiles required for the building.

Later the same tile makers must have moved to Bursa where we see the same technique for the last time in the tomb of Şehzade Mustafa built in 1474. The tomb was built for Mustafa, the beloved son of Mehmed II. The building today is also known as the tomb of Cem, another son of Mehmed II who was later buried here. The interior is decorated with gilded hexagonal monochrome tiles up to a level and a border of blue and white tiles executed in the under glaze technique frame the tiled surfaces (Fig.16 Bursa Tomb of Cem Sultan, interior).

The walls above the tiled areas are decorated with wall paintings that show floral designs arranged like oval medallions set in vases. Although quite stylized, flowers stem from the vases and the branches rise in a scrolling manner around the chinoiserie flowers of peony (*hatayi* in Turkish). The whole appears as an abstract, dense, and complex design. The floral

Fig.16 Bursa Tomb of Cem Sultan, interior

designs springing from the vases also resemble the painted decorations of the Muradiye Mosque in Edirne (see previous chapter). Such patterns were common in Timurid art in the 15th century. What is quite distinct is that the decoration of the Ottoman tomb from its tiles to wall paintings reflects an entirely Timurid taste.

Another example of eastern influenced decoration can be seen on the magnificent Tiled Pavilion (Çinili Köşk) that was built by Mehmed II as part of his New Palace (Topkapı Palace) in Istanbul (Fig. 17 Istanbul Çinili Köşk). The Tiled Pavilion was built in 1472 as a separate pavilion building to evoke Persian buildings. Not only are its architectural plan and details similar to contemporary buildings in Iran, but also its tiling on the interior and exteriors, which were the work of Iranian artists. Although one could think of this as the work of the same

Fig. 17 Istanbul Çinili Köşk

'Tabrizi artists' who worked in Bursa Green Mosque, Edirne Muradiye Mosque, and Mehmed II's Mosque in Istanbul, analysis of the tile techniques indicates that it was the work of another group of Iranian artists. The main difference is that here the *bannai* technique was used in addition to the cut tile and tile mosaic techniques. *Bannai*, which is only encountered in this building in Istanbul, required glazed tiles to be used in the actual structure of the building instead of the Ottoman building technique of cut stone and brick layers. A broad band of *bannai* tiles forming calligraphic and geometric patterns crosses the facade of the tiled kiosk and delineates its major architectural units including the main entrance at the center. The entrance itself is decorated with tile mosaics of geometric, calligraphic, and floral decoration in dark and light blue, white, yellow, and purple colors. Inside one can see hexagonal and triangular glazed tiles in turquoise, blue, and white up to a certain level. Although they were gilded over the glaze most of it has vanished.

A document in the archive of the Topkapı Palace Museum mentions Iranian tile makers who may have worked on this building. The document is a petition of Khorasani (from eastern Iran) tile cutters who were asking for further employment from Mehmed II after having completed a pavilion for him. Since there is no comparable tile work from another building in Istanbul it is assumed that these craftsmen were invited specifically to work on the Tiled Pavilion and when their work was completed they went back to their homeland.

A miniature from an Ottoman manuscript, which is roughly from the same time, (based on the style of the illuminations of the manuscript) illustrates a sultan in front of a minimally depicted tiled pavilion (see fig. 13 above). Although it is architecturally different from the Tiled Pavilion, the building in the miniature is decorated with gilded hexagonal tiles. Such gilded tiles also appear on pavilions in miniatures of another Ottoman manuscript dated to 1455 now in Oxford. Although the use of gilded hexagonal tiles have only survived from public buildings of the first half of the 15th century, we may suggest that it was probably common for Ottoman royal pavilions to be decorated with such tiles during the 15th century. As an extension of this taste artists from Iran were invited to work on the Tiled Kiosk in the sultan's palace. The miniature not only shows gilded tiles behind the seated sultan but also the blue and white ceramics of various shapes in the front. Blue and white ceramics of Chinese origin were the main inspiration behind the blue and white tiles of this era.

Ceramics

Blue and white Chinese ceramics were imported in high quantities not only by the Timurids but elsewhere in the Islamic world. As perhaps indicated by the above discussed miniature, the Ottomans must have also appreciated their porcelain-like quality, colors and shapes, such that a Chinese inspired local production of blue and white ceramics readily found patronage under the Ottomans towards the end of Mehmed II's reign. The Ottomans however did not satisfy themselves only in the copying process but created a new technique, repertoire of motifs and shapes towards the end of the 15th century. These ceramics had a hard body made with an artificial compound called frit and were covered with a white slip. The slip was painted in rich cobalt blue and then a truly transparent glaze was applied.

The technical features of these Ottoman ceramics show that they were not readily imported by the tile makers of Iran who worked in various Ottoman buildings in the 15th century. The Ottoman ceramics were made with a lead frit and the tiles of the Iranian craftsmen were made with an alkaline frit. This difference in the actual makeup suggests that this was a local Ottoman creation to satisfy the demand of the Ottoman court.

Although ceramics were produced in the first half of the 15th century in Iznik, these are made of red clay, and the shapes, decoration, and quality of the new products do not bear much of a resemblance to the old ones. While the old type of red clay ceramics continued to be produced in Iznik and a few other centers, a more expensive and labor intensive ceramic product also began to be produced in Iznik in the second half of the 15th century. Both groups were produced at different kilns by a different group of potters. While the first group satisfied the masses, the second one was strictly for the Ottoman court. In fact the second line of Iznik ceramics was most likely initially produced under the patronage of the Ottoman court. The reason for this supposition is based on the decorative repertoire of the Iznik ceramics, especially of a blue and white group.

The earliest group of Iznik ceramics is suggested to have been made only in blue and white in the 1470's and 80's, more or less in the last decade of Mehmed II's reign. In this group tightly drawn split leaves (arabesques) in white are shown over a dense cobalt blue ground. Inward turning leaves in the Baba Nakkaş style are clearly visible and when examined closely parallel hatching, which is another sign of the Baba Nakkaş style, can also be seen in the split leaves. A large dish of this type measuring 43 cm in diameter is a good example of this type (Fig. 18 Iznik dish, Istanbul Archaeological Museum, Çinili Köşk 41/8). Here the Baba Nakkaş style of inward turning leaves and fine detailing of the split leaves with parallel hatching can be seen. The central design can be compared to the illuminations of manuscripts of this period. In fact one-to-one parallels can be found in the decorations of other large blue and white dishes of this type and the illuminations and bindings of the manuscripts from the reign of Mehmed II. The blue and white lines on the interior of the Iznik dish suggest the raised on metal objects. There are other early Iznik dishes

Fig. 18 Iznik dish, Istanbul Archaeological Museum, Çinili Köşk 41/8

that copy metalwork shapes and decoration as well. Based on this connection with the metalwork, scholars suggested that Iznik potters were trying to produce the shapes of metalwork in ceramic since the Ottomans were accustomed to using silver vessels. The costly Iznik ceramics would have complemented the silver vessels, which were already used in the palace kitchens and supply further need for vessels. Kitchen registers of the Ottoman court dated to 1489-90 are proof that Iznik pottery was purchased by the Ottoman court although their number had still not surpassed those of silver objects.

Another group of blue and white ceramics is attributed to the reign of Bayezid II (1481-1512). Although the overall decoration is quite similar to the previous group, the individual motifs begin to be placed more spaciously over a lighter blue ground. This creates a less dense impression and perhaps facilitates the painting process of the ceramics. A mosque lamp (Fig. 19 Iznik mosque lamp, Istanbul Archeological Museum, Çinili Köşk 41/6) that came from the tomb of Bayezid II in

Istanbul exemplifies this style. Here the floral decorations are complemented with calligraphic cartouches where the words of God (Allah), Muhammed (the Prophet) and Ali (caliph and cousin of the Prophet) are written (in the middle cartouche). A cloud-inspired design can be seen on the neck with elaborate designs of knots. The combination of calligraphy with knots and cloud-inspired designs is visible in contemporary Ottoman illumination and bindings as well. Ceramic mosque lamps must have been produced in high quantities since the new mosques and tombs built in Istanbul after the conquest would have required such furnishings.

Large footed basins were a new creation of the Iznik potters possibly at the end of the 15th century. These large vessels with diameters of around 45cm were most likely made from molds and the same design was applied on a few of them. Although the earliest surviving examples of footed bowls of this type are dated circa 1510, the opening page of an Ottoman manuscript dated to 1499 (New York, Metropolitan Museum of Art) shows a footed basin of this type. In this miniature the food is carried in various blue and white dishes by Ottoman court officials in front of the Ottoman sultan. The large blue and white footed basin appears to have been used for serving food as well. The miniature indicates that the footed basins were used as early as 1499 at the Ottoman court.

Fig. 19 Iznik mosque lamp, Istanbul Archeological Museum, Çinili Köşk 41/6)

The complex designs of the blue and white group directly relate them to the court studio. The craftsmen who executed these designs on the ceramics must have been skilled artists who could apply the court designs on these ceramics. The ceramic lamps which were produced for the mosques and tombs of the Ottoman sultan and his entourage also indicate that this blue and white group was made specifically for the Ottoman court.

In addition to Iznik, Kütahya, a city in western Anatolia, also began to produce ceramics in blue and white. A blue and white ewer with an Armenian inscription on its base mentions that it was made by Abraham of Kütahya in 1510. Compared to the above mentioned blue and white ceramics for court use the style of painting on this ewer is rather crude and most likely represents an example of non-imperial and non-Muslim patronage that was taking place in Kütahya. Based on this dated example we can surmise that by 1510 blue and white Iznik products had already attained a reputation to be replicated at other Ottoman ceramic centers.

Metalwork

Ottoman sultans and high court officials were fond of valuable metal objects especially gold and silver for their use in the palace. Although Islamic religious customs forbade the use of these metals, the Ottomans did not stick to this rule just like many other Islamic courts. Some of these gold and silver objects were collected as booty as Ottomans conquered various cities in the west and east. The Ottomans also acquired the silver and gold mines of the Balkans. Unfortunately few metal objects have survived from the 15th century. Since such metals were particularly valuable when the court was in financial stress a high quantity must have been melted and reused as coins. As mentioned earlier Iznik ceramics were imitating certain metalwork shapes and designs, and court records from 1489-90 mention the high number of silver vessels in the kitchens. Some objects from the public realm allow us to see some of the features of Ottoman metalwork during the second half of the 15th century. A silver lantern from the mosque of Mehmed II (Fig. 20 Mosque lantern, Istanbul Turkish and Islamic Arts Museum, 167) made in the 1460's, clearly shows that designs of the court studio could be applied to metalwork as well. The lantern consists of six sides, each decorated with a lobed central medallion with arabesques spiraling from the center, which are also pierced. The size of the central medallion and the piercing of its surface resemble book binding decorations of the period, which were made using a similar technique called filigree. On the book bindings the central oval design is pierced on the thin leather surface revealing a colored surface beneath it.

Two large candlesticks from the mosque of Bayezid II in Edirne built in 1487 are made of gilded bronze,

Fig. 20 Mosque lantern, Istanbul Turkish and Islamic Arts Museum, 167

although the gilding is largely rubbed off (Fig. 21 Mosque Candlestick, Istanbul Turkish and Islamic Arts Museum, 139a-b). Such candlesticks were placed on both sides of the prayer niche (*mihrab*) in Ottoman mosques to symbolize the holy light coming from the direction of Mecca. These particular candlesticks have large calligraphic bands that praise the light coming from the candlestick. The inscription in Persian also states that they were made for Bayezid II in Edirne. Around the calligraphy small leaves in the Baba Nakkaş style spread to the ground show that the Baba Nakkaş style was applied also to metalwork. Almost identical candlesticks from Bayezid's mosque in Amasya (completed in 1486) most likely indicate that all four candlesticks were made at the same time.

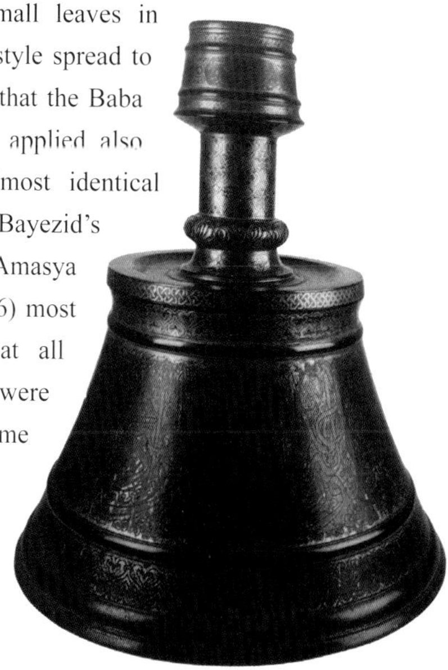

Fig.21 Mosque Candlestick, Istanbul Turkish and Islamic Arts Museum, 139a-b

Carpets

Although we begin to see the dissemination of court designs in Ottoman carpets towards the end of the 15th century on a group of carpets, other types of carpets which do not show any resemblance were also produced in the second half of the 15th century. In fact some of them may have been produced even before that date. Although Ottoman carpets are difficult to date within the 15th century, carpets of this century were reproduced in European paintings of 15th and early 16th century artists such as the Dutch artist Hans Holbein and the Italian artists Lorenzo Lotto, Giovanni Bellini, and Gentile Bellini. Carpets of certain designs are dated with more certainty based on these European paintings. Three main types are observed: The so-called Holbein carpets have repeating large octagons or smaller squares delineated with knots. The ground is usually dark blue or red. The earliest appearance of this type of carpet in a European painting is 1451. The second group, the so-called Lotto carpets, displays small repeating floriate motifs that vaguely form a diamond shape. Their yellow grounds distinguish them from the Holbein types. Their earliest appearance in a European painting is 1509. Since the Lotto group has a floral aspect, they may have begun to be produced sometime after the Holbein group. The third group, the so-called Bellini carpets, shows a pattern in the shape of a large keyhole in the main field. Red or blue colors are common. The Ottoman towns of Uşak and Bergama in western Turkey and perhaps Konya in central Turkey are thought to be the production centers for the three carpet types which were largely exported. However like the animal carpets produced earlier (see previous chapter) the so called Holbein, Lotto and Bellini carpets continued to be made for a long time and perhaps in many more places than just the initial centers.

The other type of carpets where we see Ottoman court designs is also attributed to Uşak. However their complex designs and large sizes completely differ from the previous carpets. One group known as 'Medallion Uşak' carpets has a large medallion in the center and quarter medallions in the corners (Fig. 22 Carpet, Istanbul Turkish and Islamic Arts Museum, 4). The areas between the medallions are also decorated with detailed floral motifs. The ground is usually dark blue or red. The other related group, known as 'Star Uşak' carpets, is also close in design. Here the medallions are more in the shape of a star. The sizes of these carpets reached more than 7m in length. Such curvilinear and floral motifs in addition to their large sizes, which are so different from those of earlier carpets, must have required the weavers to set up new looms and rely on cartoons to execute them. Thus scholars suggest that this was accomplished only with the direct intervention of the Ottoman court. The decorative repertoire of the carpets also supports this view. All the stylized floral motifs used in and around the medallions are common in manuscript illuminations and bindings of the 1460's and 1470's made during the reign of Mehmed II. While the book bindings display more of the empty zone between the center and corner medallions, the carpets emphasize the medallions and decrease the space between the

Fig. 22 Carpet, Istanbul Turkish and Islamic Arts Museum, 4

center and corner pieces. In both groups the spaces between the medallions are filled with a spray of small floral motifs also seen on Ottoman and Timurid illuminations. Especially the 'oak leaf' palmet type can be seen in the decorations attributed to Baba Nakkaş (see fig.10), and ceramics of the period. During the 1460's important architectural undertakings were taking place in Istanbul. The New Palace (Topkapı Palace) and the large mosque complex of Mehmed were being completed. Large size Uşak carpets with new designs could have been the result of Mehmed's initiative to produce equally ambitious objects suitable for these new buildings. It is documented that Mehmed II had court carpet-weavers. Thus the very initial carpets of the new type could have been produced at the court with the direct transition from cartoons to the carpets. Then necessary equipment and material could have been set up in Uşak to produce more of the same type of carpets. Like the other types of carpets discussed above, the medallion and Star Uşak carpets continued to be made for a long time. The earliest appearance of Uşak carpets is in a painting called *Return of the Ring to the Doge* by Paris Bordone dated to 1534. Today the Turkish and Islamic arts Museum in Istanbul display a variety of such carpets.

Woodwork

Among the few surviving specimens of the woodwork of the period, the doors of the present day treasury hall of the Topkapı Palace, which was originally built during the reign of Mehmed II, are a good example of the Baba Nakkaş style applied on wood (Fig. 23 Detail of doors from the treasury hall known as Fatih Köşkü, Topkapı Palace Museum). Here we can see the inward turning leaves and the lobed split leaves in relief commonly applied on ceramics as a painting. While the traditional motifs and compositions continue on woodwork, new innovative style of Baba Nakkaş which was inspired after the Chinese-Timurid designs reflects the widely applied esthetic taste of the Ottoman court at that time.

Fig. 23 Detail of door from the treasury hall known as Fatih Köşkü, Topkapı Palace Museum

Chapter 4

The development and organization of the court workshops (1512-1566)

Historical setting

The reigns of Selim I and Süleyman I were dominated by an ever-increasing Ottoman military and political power. Selim who reigned from 1512 to 1520 usurped the throne from his father Bayezid II, despite the fact that Bayezid openly declared his wish for his other son Ahmed's succession. Selim became the Ottoman sultan at the age of 45 after a long time as a governor in Trabzon. After eliminating his brothers and their sons during the first year of his reign Selim employed a rather aggressive policy in Ottoman military activities unlike his father's stabilizing policies. Selim marched against his rival Shah Ismail in Iran. He defeated the Shah's army in 1514 and entered the court city of Tabriz. After staying there a week Selim left with a great deal of booty as well as artists, artisans, and rich merchants.

In the following years, Selim made advances in the southeast region of Anatolia. After conquering the principality of the Dhul-Kadiri, the Mamluks, who controlled Syria and Egypt, opposed Ottoman advances in this region. Selim declared war against them and won victories in two major battles in 1516 and 1517 and entered Cairo. Like in Tabriz he brought a large booty and trained men back to the Ottoman capital. He is considered to have assumed the Islamic caliphate from the Mamluks, and after Selim, Ottoman sultans considered themselves as the Caliph of all Muslims. This had long-term implications for the Ottoman sultans. After the fall of the Mamluks, the Sharifs of

Mecca and Yemen also accepted Ottoman control and the two holy cities of Islam, Mecca and Medina, came under Ottoman control.

Selim maintained good relations with European countries during his years of conquest in the east. However, in 1519 he prepared a large navy, possibly to conquer Rhodes and Chios, but died on 21 September 1520 before achieving his goals. His only son, Süleyman (the Magnificent), succeeded him. At the end of his reign Selim doubled the size of the empire by conquering lands of other Muslim territories, unlike his predecessors who made advances mostly against the Christian dominated regions in Europe.

Selim, who was born and trained in the Amasya palace during his father's governorate in this city, spent 22 years as a governor of Trabzon before he ascended throne. Although he spent a long time on campaign he also enjoyed reading history and literature. His Persian poems are collected as an album. Several *Selimnames* explaining the history of his time were written during his reign.

Süleyman, Selim's only living son ascended the throne in 1520 at the age of 26 without any struggle unlike his predecessors. He first tried to rehabilitate the people who suffered from his father's harsh policies and created new laws to protect life, property, and honor. Thus he is known in Ottoman sources as 'law maker' (Kanuni). After quelling internal rebellions he moved to the west towards Hungary, which refused to pay the annual tribute. He conquered Belgrade in 1521. Then he moved towards the Aegean islands and captured Rhodes in 1522 from the Knights of St. John in order to secure the sea connection between Istanbul and Egypt. When the mother of the French emperor Francis I asked the Ottoman sultan to help with the release of his son who was held by the holy Roman emperor, Süleyman became closely involved in European politics. Süleyman immediately attacked Hungary, which was held by the Austrian Habsburgs, the rivals of the French. This resulted in the Ottoman victory at Mohac in 1526. The Ottomans continued to be involved with European politics and the rivalry between the Habsburgs and the French until 1533 when Süleyman made truce with the Austrian Habsburgs. In the Mediterranean, the Ottoman navy began to assert its power mainly after the victorious battle of Preveza in 1538. Algeria came under Ottoman control in 1533. In the east Süleyman made two major campaigns in 1533-35 and 1548-55 against the Safavids ruled by Shah Tahmasb. As a result, he conquered the cities of Tabriz and Baghdad and annexed Georgia. The Ottoman navy also made successful gains in the Red Sea towards the south and Aden (Yemen) became an Ottoman province. After the conquest of Basra in Iraq, Suez and Basra became the main naval bases for Ottoman operations in the Indian Ocean. Süleyman died in his old age during a campaign against Szigetvar in Hungary in 1566. At the end of Süleyman's long reign, the Ottoman territorial expansion spread to three continents.

Süleyman, who was born in Trabzon, received a good training in the Islamic tradition in his childhood. He governed the cities of Şebinkarahisar, Bolu, Kefe, and Manisa. During his time as a prince in Kefe and Manisa he had a large staff of artists. Süleyman's early years of his long reign (66 years) was a period of pomp and splendor that gave him the title 'Magnificent' in Europe. Süleyman legally married his consort Hürrem in 1534 who gave birth to four sons. Şehzade Mehmed was chosen by his parents as the heir and he enjoyed popularity at the court but he passed away in 1543. By the late 1540's Süleyman's health began to deteriorate and he became more religious. He began to worry about the religious correctness of his actions. He gave up silver and gold tableware and used only Chinese porcelain for personal use. He made a total of 13 campaigns during his reign. He wrote poetry under the penname Muhibbi (the affectionate) and his poems constitute a large album.

Architectural activity

The building activity during Selim's time was limited due to his long military campaigns. After his Egyptian campaign he brought craftsmen from Cairo with the intention of building a *medrese* decorated with marble revetments in the Cairo style. These craftsmen are known to have worked after Selim's unexpected death on the marble decoration of some sections of the Topkapı Palace and the vizier Çoban Mustafa's Mosque in Gebze, near Istanbul. Selim also began a mosque complex in Istanbul although his son Süleyman completed it in 1527.

Major architectural activity took place during the reign of Süleyman. Most of this activity falls under the tenure of the chief architect Sinan. Sinan became the chief court architect in 1539 after humble beginnings as a Christian recruit (*devşirme*) from Kayseri, a town in Turkey. According to this system young Christian boys were recruited from their families to be trained for military and various services at the Ottoman court. The system required these boys to abandon most family ties and achieve a Muslim-Ottoman identity. Sinan was first trained in carpentry, and then in building and engineering. When Sinan joined the Ottoman army in its various campaigns during the reigns of Selim and Süleyman in Hungary, Iraq, Azerbaijan, Iran, Corfu, Italy, and Moldavia, he rigorously improved his skills in engineering over a period of twenty years. After proving his skills in the army he became the chief architect after Alauddin known as Ali of Persia died. As chief architect he spent another 50 years working on numerous buildings and projects. His numerous mosque complexes built for Süleyman, his wife Hürrem, daughter, and sons (For Sultan Selim II and his son Murad III see the next chapter) reflect the architectural supremacy Sinan achieved in his long career as a court architect. Not only did he design many buildings as an architect but he also supervised building activity all over the empire as an administrator and architect. He was even responsible for building regulations, water supply for the city, and repair of public monuments.

The Haseki Mosque complex built by Süleyman for his mother in 1539 was the first of Sinan's such buildings in Istanbul. Sinan's first major monument was built for Şehzade (prince) Mehmed who died at the young age of 21. The mosque complex of Şehzade Mehmed was built by Sinan for the beloved son of Süleyman in four years and completed in 1548. In this mosque Sinan achieved a large centralized space with a main dome supported by four half domes in a square plan. The two minarets of the mosque are decorated with stone work. The Süleymaniye Mosque complex, which was completed in 1559, was architecturally one of Sinan's best works. (The mosque was finished in 1557 and more additions including Hürrem's tomb, *medreses,* and water channels were finished in 1559. Süleyman's own tomb was finished in 1568.) The massive complex included a mosque, tombs, *medreses*, hospital, medical school, soup kitchen, caravanserai, Koran school, and a bath. An average of 3000 people worked daily on the construction of the complex. All the resources of the empire were made available to Sinan to use for the complex. It became the largest social and religious center of the empire. The mosque's plan with a large central dome and two supporting half domes repeats that of the Bayezid Mosque but in a much larger scale. Its massive triangular and cascading structure from outside and the four minarets still dominate Istanbul's landscape.

Sinan built two mosques for Süleyman's daughter in Üsküdar (1548) and Edirnekapı. The one in Edirnekapı completed in 1565 displays Sinan's architectural ingenuity with a single dome raised above window-pierced walls. In fact several medium-sized mosques built by Sinan in Istanbul and other cities for the viziers and high-level court officials display his architectural creativity in the use of available land, airy centralized interiors, and harmonious decorative programs. Among them Kara Ahmed Pasha and Rüstem Pasha Mosques were built during the reign of Süleyman.

Süleyman also built and restored several buildings on the Hajj route. Every year, as now, devout Muslims visited the holy site of Kaaba and its environs in Mecca. When Mecca and Medina came under Ottoman control after Selim I, the Ottoman sultans considered it a prestige to renovate the holy sanctuaries and its furnishings. Thus Süleyman redecorated the Dome of the Rock in Jerusalem, the first monument of Islam dated to 691 and built a mosque and a *medrese* in Damascus.

Decorative arts

This period was one of the most prolific times in history for Ottoman decorative arts. During the reign of Süleyman artistic norms that future Ottoman art heavily depended on were established, and the period is thus considered classical in many respects.

Although Selim I's reign was merely eight years, and he spent most of his time on campaign away from the Ottoman capital, his military activities made a large impact on the arts of the following periods, especially in the development of the court studio, the *nakkaşhane*. The contemporary historian Şükri Beg of Bitlis records that when Selim entered Tabriz 2000 families of artists and artisans were sent to Istanbul from

Tabriz. In his account Şükri Bey explains that Selim gave orders to bring all the treasures and valuable objects as well as scholars, artists, and merchants so that the Ottomans would not need Persians in such matters. When Selim conquered Tabriz in 1514, the Safavid court had already amassed skilled artists of the book and a rich collection of luxury manuscripts from the Akkoyunlu and Timurid courts when they had invaded Tabriz in 1502 and Herat in 1510. Consequently, the booty brought from Tabriz by Selim included several of the luxury manuscripts of those courts as well. Badi al-Zaman who was the son of the last Timurid ruler in Herat was living in Tabriz and welcomed Selim when he entered the city. Selim duly respected the prince and allowed him to come to Istanbul with his retinue and also provided an income for him. His arrival at the Ottoman court with his retinue of artists who originally came from Herat is thought to have influenced Ottoman arts of the book. Tile makers of Tabriz and carpet weavers of Tabriz and Cairo also contributed to the Ottoman arts of this period.

During the last years of Selim's short reign and in the earlier part of Süleyman's long reign, Ottoman imperial workshops were flooded with trained artists, who were brought by Selim from Tabriz, Aleppo, Damascus, and Cairo after his conquests. Newly recruited apprentices also joined the court workshops. These court workshops, including the court studio, were organized to reflect these changes during the reign of Süleyman. The results were spectacular in many ways and new creations were made by local and emigrant artists working together under the patronage of the Ottoman sultan. While the earlier part of Süleyman's reign was marked by the creations of the craftsmen from Iran, the latter part was marked by the recruited craftsmen who received most of their training in the Ottoman workshops and worked side by side with the Iranian masters.

The Ottoman court artists were organized according to the crafts they performed. All were regarded as part of the royal household and palace administration. Their divisions were as high as fifty and included painter-designers, binders, jewelers, goldsmiths, tailors, ceramic and tile makers, embroiderers, carpet and textile weavers, makers of silver thread, and makers of swords among many others. The head treasurer of the palace was in charge of all the divisions. The raw materials, especially valuable ones, were distributed by him to the craftsmen. The total number of craftsmen was about 600 during Süleyman's reign. The craftsmen could have been included into the system based on their proven skills in a certain area, like the artists who came from Tabriz, or they could have been selected as recruits who were then trained and promoted if they showed improving signs of artistic talent. The court paid them daily wages, which were given every three months. The master artists were given monthly salaries. In addition to their daily wages, which were perhaps not much, the artists were able to increase their wages considerably by presenting gifts to the sultan on religious holidays and other important days. For the gifts they presented they either received cash or valuable robes or sometimes both from the sultan. Generally the court workshops were able to handle relatively small-scale productions and for larger court orders commercial workshops in the city or in the provinces were employed. But regulations were imposed even to the commercial ones. The court workshops excelled in high technical quality and aesthetic achievements and through a centralized system it became a model for all Ottoman arts.

Decorated manuscripts and works on paper

The court studio (*nakkaşhane*) made a large impact on the output of the other court workshops by providing them designs. The earliest surviving payroll register of the court studio dated to 1526 gives the number of painter-designers that were already taken during the reign of Bayezid II as nine and the new ones that joined after Selim's conquests as thirteen. Nineteen new ones must have joined the studio during the reign of Süleyman. All of the artists totaling forty-one were directed by a Tabrizi master called Şah Kulu. Beyond Tabrizi artists, two Circassian, one Albanian, and one Moldavian artist are recorded. This shows that during Süleyman's reign artists originating from the Balkan and Northern provinces of the empire were also recruited. The court studio grew even larger in time. A register from 1545 reports the number of artists working for the court studio as 59. There were two subgroups called *Rumiyan* (Anatolian) and *Aceman* (Persian) most likely according to their recruitment type. This division continued through the1560's when the Iranian masters died or became old and the recruited apprentices became masters themselves.

Şah Kulu who was a recruit from Iran became the head of the court studio after Hasan Çelebi who was in this position during the last years of Bayezid II's reign, Selim's entire reign and the early reign of Süleyman. Şah Kulu most likely came after Selim I's conquest of Tabriz. He was working as a salaried artist already in 1526. Interestingly although he was probably from Iran he is recorded as head of the *Rumiyan* division of the studio in 1545. Perhaps no one among the recruits was high enough to lead this division. In 1566 when he died he is recorded as the head of the entire studio. A 16th century Ottoman historian notes that Süleyman personally visited Şah Kulu and watched him work. Palace records indicate that Şah Kulu presented several gifts to the sultan and received large gifts as recompense from Süleyman. He is also known as a poet who wrote under the penname Penahi.

Şah Kulu's own artistic creativity and the artists working with Şah Kulu produced the second blooming Ottoman style: *saz* (Reed) style. Şah Kulu's creative style spread to various arts, just like Baba Nakkaş style did, much before he was appointed as the head of the court studio. Şah Kulu's drawings in the *saz* style are executed with ink on paper with occasional details in gold and light color washes. They mainly consist of large stylized serrated leaves in addition to peonies. The compositions sometimes resemble reed plants cast away with the wind. The leaves twist and turn and sometimes animals like lions, rabbits, and deer as well as fantastic animals are shown within this foliage. Instead of a central or repeating modular designs the artist can arrange the motifs in any way he wishes more like a canvas painting. The details in many *saz* style drawings are so minute that the artists must have used a magnifying glass while executing them. Many drawings by Şah Kulu himself or other fellow artists working in his style are today found as single drawings in albums in the Topkapı collection but also in various museums and collections in Europe and the US. A drawing from such an album (Fig. 24 Album page, Topkapı Palace Museum, H. 2147, 32a), shows a lion and a dragon in combat amidst thick foliage. The spines of the animal figures are outlined in dark in such a way to suggest third dimension. The foliage includes detailed drawings of peonies (*hatayi*) and birds hidden behind the leaves and branches.

Fig. 24 Album page, Topkapı Palace Museum, H. 2147, 32a

Beyond such designs the court studio continued to produce decorated manuscripts for the sultan and his entourage. In general we see that the artists who came from Tabriz brought their own tastes as well. One of the few Ottoman manuscripts that can be attributed to Selim's reign is a 1515 copy of the Persian literary classic, *Mantik al-Tayr* by Attar (Fig. 25 *Mantik al-Tayr* of Attar, Topkapı Palace Museum EH. 1512, 22b-23a). In this book we see the Persian taste of the artists in many respects. First of all, the miniature style that is applied here does not include any European elements that we began to see in Ottoman miniatures from the reign of Bayezid. The brush technique is quite refined and decorative elements common in contemporary Persian miniatures are visible in gilded skies, costumes, and thrones. Second, all the miniatures are arranged as double page miniatures (total of eight double-page compositions) with extra decorations on the margins. Some of these marginal decorations bear the favorite decorative elements of the Ottoman court studio such as the triple dot and

Fig. 25 Mantik al-Tayr of Attar, Topkapı Palace Museum EH. 1512, 22b-23a

wavy line motif called *çintemani*. Overall a more luxurious level was introduced even if the number of miniatures was not very high. The use of double-page compositions for all the miniatures of this manuscript, the style itself, and the full decoration of the margins signal the higher standards for luxury that were brought by the Persian artists to the production of Ottoman illustrated manuscripts.

We see that a style close to the miniatures of the *Mantik al-Tayr* was applied on the illustrations of a few other manuscripts until the 1550's at the Ottoman court studio. Selim I's own collection of poetry (*divan*) written in Persian was also illustrated in this style.

We see that artists, who came from Iran, usually kept their styles but we know that at least one artist Pir Ahmed bin Iskender, who came from Iran, began to include in his works some elements that were favored at the Ottoman court. He was a binder, calligrapher, illuminator, and illustrator, as we understand from his own words written at the end of a manuscript dated to 1530. In 1515 perhaps when he had first arrived at the Ottoman court from Tabriz, he worked on a small manuscript in Turkish by the late 15th century Turkish writer Hamdi. The manuscript was illustrated with six miniatures in the Persian style. In 1530 Pir Ahmed worked on Ali Şir Nevai's *Hamse*, a Chagatai-Turkish work that was a favorite both at the Timurid court

Fig. 26 Hamse of Ali Şir Nevai, Topkapı Palace Museum, H. 802, 66b

Fig. 27 Hamse of Ali Şir Nevai, Topkapı Palace Museum, H.802, binding

of Husain Baykara in Herat (present day Afghanistan) in the late 15th century and at the Ottoman court in Süleyman's time (Fig. 26 *Hamse* of Ali Şir Nevai, Topkapı Palace Museum, H. 802, 66b). In this manuscript he made sumptuous illuminations in dark blue and gold displaying his virtuosity in this area, and 16 miniatures. From 1515 to 1530 we see that his style began to change and included some perspectival elements in architecture and also light and dark tones to indicate the third dimension. Pir Ahmed also made an exquisite binding in the *saz* style for this manuscript (Fig. 27 *Hamse* of Ali Şir Nevai, Topkapı Palace Museum, H.802, binding). The lacquer binding is decorated with Şah Kulu style *saz* leaves and foliage in red outlines with gold over a black ground. Its lacquer technique allowed Pir Ahmed to apply a painterly style like the ink drawings of Şah Kulu on a binding. The application of fine serrated leaves on this 1530 binding is proof that other artists at the court studio were applying Şah Kulu style designs already by this date. As we will see below Şah Kulu's *saz* style disseminated to all other media in a short time and continued to be repeated in various forms in the next centuries.

A second style that spread from the court studio to other arts of the period was created by Mehmed Çelebi known as Kara Memi. An apprentice of Şah Kulu, Kara Memi became the head of the court studio after Şah Kulu died in 1556. According to extent court records Kara Memi had worked in the court studio at least from 1540 to 1566. Contrary to Şah Kulu, Kara Memi is only known for his work as an illuminator on manuscripts. However his style also spread to other court arts like textiles and tiles. Kara Memi's style introduced a new vocabulary to Ottoman illumination. It includes naturalistic garden flowers and new color combinations. Although unsigned, a religious manuscript on the sayings of the Prophet Muhammad displays the use of Kara Memi style flowers on the binding and the illumination (Fig. 28 Forty *Hadith*, Topkapı Palace Museum, EH. 2851, interior binding). Just as Pir Ahmed applied Şah Kulu style *saz* leaves on an earlier lacquered binding, Kara Memi style flowers were applied on the lacquer binding of this manuscript dedicated to Şehzade Mehmed who was the beloved son of

Fig. 28 Forty Hadith, Topkapı Palace Museum, EH. 2851, interior binding

Süleyman and died in 1543. In fact Kara Memi himself may have executed the lacquer binding. The interior of this binding with colorful carnations, roses, hyacinths, and tulips display Kara Memi's emerging and innovative style. The illuminations also include the same repertoire but more hesitantly in the margins above the standard title decoration. It appears that in the 1540's Kara Memi practiced his new style perhaps as a trial side by side with traditional motifs. The calligraphy which is entirely executed from cutout paper (*kaatı*) belongs to the skilled Benli Ali Çelebi, who signed his work at the end of the manuscript. Known as a work of art itself all the letters are cut out from white paper and pasted on colored paper. This exceptionally talented artist, who was a recruit from Buda, worked on several manuscripts for Süleyman.

A poetry album dated to 1566 and signed by Kara Memi as the illuminator shows his repertoire in full bloom (Fig. 29 *Divan-ı Muhibbi*, Istanbul University Library, 5467, 359b-360a). The poems belong to Süleyman himself and Süleyman is declared as a ruler and a poet at the beginning of this manuscript in illuminated medallions. Kara Memi's signature at the end of the

Fig. 29 Divan-ı Muhibbi, Istanbul University Library, 5467, 359b-360a

manuscript as an illuminator signals his established career. In this manuscript the main illumination around the text includes tulips, hyacinths, and carnations in various colors. The marginal decorations in the *saz* style complete the decoration.

Although unsigned, Kara Memi may have worked on an interim manuscript, a Koran dedicated to Süleyman and dated to 1546-47. (Fig. 30 Koran, Topkapı Palace Museum, YY 999, 1b- 2a). Here Kara Memi style flowers decorate the background of the first and seventh lines of the text and narrow vertical areas on both sides of the text block. Other areas are illuminated in the traditional style seen on manuscripts of Bayezid II's reign. This Koran is copied by the most celebrated calligrapher of

Fig. 30 Koran, Topkapı Palace Museum, YY 999, 1b- 2a

Süleyman's time, Ahmed Karahisari. Ahmed Karahisari (d. 1556) who was from the town of Afyon Karahisar in Turkey introduced greater dynamism to the already established calligraphic letterforms of the Yakut school. He was a student of the famous Persian calligrapher Kirmani. He copied many Korans now preserved in the museum collections in Turkey. Karahisari's many calligraphic designs have a modern appeal as well (Fig. 31 *En'am*, Istanbul Turkish and Islamic Arts Museum, 1443, 1b). Although Karahisari was well respected during his life time only seven calligraphers followed in his footsteps and his style practically died out in the early 17th century in favor of that of Şeyh Hamdullah, who was the most famous calligrapher of the second half of the 15th century. Hasan Çelebi, also named Hasan bin Ahmed Karahisari (d. after 1594), was Karahisari's immediate student and adopted son. His famous work from this period was the calligraphic decorations of the Süleymaniye Mosque.

Fig. 31 En'am, Istanbul Turkish and Islamic Arts Museum, 1443, 1b

Another area where we see the output of the imperial calligraphers and illuminators is imperial monograms of the Ottoman sultans. *Tuğras*, which were affixed on official administrative papers such as decrees to indicate authenticity, were specifically designed for each Ottoman sultan although some basic guidelines were followed. This complex calligraphic monogram consisted of the sultan's name, his patronymics, his title, and a formulaic wish for victory. The *tuğras* were affixed by a certain court officer called *nişancı* but important documents were affixed with *tuğras* that were also decorated by court illuminators. Such *tuğras* show some of the best

Fig. 32 Ferman, Topkapı Palace Museum Archive, E. 7816/2

illuminations of their time. A decree dated to April 16, 1552 (Fig. 32 *Ferman*, Topkapı Palace Museum Archive, E. 7816/2) indicates the grant of lands in Lebanon and an income from Süleyman to his wife Hürrem. The *tuğra* is decorated with saz leaves as well as carnations in the Kara Memi style.

The appearance of the Kara Memi style in other illuminated manuscripts and decorations in other media show that Kara Memi's naturalistic style was influential on a variety of decorative arts of the period just like those of Baba Nakkaş and Şah Kulu.

The court studio produced several illustrated manuscripts during the reign of Süleyman. Interestingly a large group was connected to the military activities of the Ottoman sultans. These historical works were meant to document the great military achievement of the Ottoman sultans both in writing and illustration. Süleyman's reign was of course a victorious period of Ottoman military expansion and his interest in documenting such accomplishments was quite understandable. An artist from Bosnia, Nasuh Bosnavi (also known as Nasuh Matrakçı) is known to have written and illustrated histories of Bayezid II, Selim I, and Süleyman at the order of Süleyman. He joined Süleyman on his 1534 Iranian campaign and created a book with illustrations of the places the army passed through, almost like a guidebook. His images of various cities like Istanbul, Aleppo, include no humans but provide the geographic and architectural highlights of them. The famous picture of Istanbul (Fig. 33 *Mecmu'i Menazil*, Istanbul University Library, T 5964, 8b-9a) shows the large city within the city walls, the golden horn and the smaller settlement in Galata. Various viewpoints are chosen for the depiction of the city, which is typical for Nasuh. Major monuments of the city such as the Topkapı Palace, Hagia Sophia, Hippodrome (At Meydanı) and its monuments, the *Arslanhane* (converted church used as the court studio), the Old palace, the Mosque of Mehmed II, and the Galata Tower are clearly depicted.

Fig. 33 Mecmu'i Menazil, Istanbul University Library, T 5964, 8b-9a

Beginning with Nasuh, history writing gained importance for the Ottomans and in 1541 a special post was created for an Iranian poet at the Ottoman court known as Arifi, who produced five volumes of Ottoman history in Persian. He tried to emulate the famous Iranian epic *Şahname* (*Shahnama*) in its literary style. The volumes started from Adam and continued with the lives of the Prophets. The third volume was devoted to the history of the first Ottoman rulers until Bayezid I. The fifth volume named the *Süleymanname* was reserved for Süleyman's own reign until 1558 when the copy was completed. These copies were illustrated by the most accomplished court painters, who displayed different styles in their illustrations. While some illustrations were in the more typical Persian style, some were in the Ottoman style, which included perspectival drawings and shadows. The creation of these volumes shows that Süleyman was trying to vie with the past Iranian rulers and place his ancestry and himself while still alive as part of this history. These five volumes with numerous illustrations are not only valuable for their literary and aesthetic merit but also for their documentation of the Ottoman court, its administration and social life. (Fig. 34 *Süleymanname,* Topkapı Palace Museum, H. 1517, 360a). A miniature in this manuscript depicts Süleyman receiving Barbaros, the famed seaman of Algiers, who would become the chief Ottoman admiral and lead the Ottoman navy. In order to greet Süleyman, Barbaros

Fig. 34 Süleymanname, Topkapı Palace Museum, H. 1517, 360a

brought hundreds of prisoners carrying valuables, female slaves dressed in silks, camels loaded with gifts, and rare animals. Barbaros and his admirals followed them in modest clothes. In the miniature while Süleyman and other court officials are shown wearing luxury caftans, Barbaros who was sixty-three years old at that time is shown wearing a plain caftan as told in the text. The binding of the manuscript is the first luxury example of the *saz* style on an Ottoman binding. The exterior of the binding continues the formulations of the previous century in its general scheme: a central medallion and four corner pieces. But the details of the decoration include new motifs. The front and back covers are decorated with a gilded oval medallion in the center and four corner pieces, and a large gilded band surrounds the inner frame. All the gilded areas are decorated with serrated *saz* leaves and *hatayis*. Overall the gilded areas contrast sharply with the empty areas. The interior of the binding shows more of the empty zones in burgundy between the gilded central medallion and the four corner pieces (Fig. 35 *Süleymanname*, Topkapı Palace Museum, H. 1517 interior binding). Here in addition to the *saz* style motifs, cloud

Fig. 35 Süleymanname, Topkapı Palace Museum, H. 1517 interior binding

bands, which entered the Ottoman decorative repertoire during the reign of Bayezid, can also be seen. The ratios between the design units, the decorative motifs, and color schemes seen on this manuscript became typical of the classical style and are repeatedly applied up to the 20th century. Although unsigned, Mehmed Çelebi, who was the head of the binders during the reign of Süleyman, was most likely responsible for the execution of this important manuscript.

Architectural decoration

Various examples of tile decoration, especially from the reign of Süleyman display the major styles of Ottoman decorative arts. We know that Selim brought at least three tile cutters from Tabriz. One of them, Habib of Tabriz became the head of the court workshop of tiles in Istanbul by 1526 with ten apprentices working for him. Although Habib was from Tabriz, his assistants were from the Balkan and Anatolian cities. Ali, one of Habib's assistants, became the head of the workshop in 1527, perhaps when Habib died. This group of artisans was paid by the Ottoman court on a regular basis and they specifically catered to the needs of the court. Their workshops were not on the palace grounds but most likely in the Tekfur Sarayı district of Istanbul. They reintroduced eastern fashions such as the

Fig. 36 Chamber of petitions cuerda seca tiles, Topkapı Palace Museum

cuerda seca technique back into the Ottoman repertoire and were responsible for several buildings decorated with tiles in the first half of the 16th century.

The mosque and tomb of Selim, which was built between 1520 and 1527 by Süleyman in Istanbul in honor of his father, were decorated by these Tabrizi craftsmen. The tiled window arches made in the *cuerda seca* technique from the Mosque of Selim show that these craftsmen used designs based on Timurid models and earlier 15th century Ottoman examples from Bursa and Edirne.

The same type of *cuerda seca* tiles also appear in a few places in the Topkapı Palace: the arches of the interior windows of the circumcision room (*sünnet odası*), the facade of chamber of petitions (*arz odası*), (Fig. 36 Chamber of petitions *cuerda seca* tiles, Topkapı Palace Museum), and inside the Baghdad and Revan kiosks. All of these buildings were either renovated or built after Süleyman's time but the older *cuerda secca* tiles were included in the new buildings or reassembled in a new fashion. A careful study of the buildings, their history, and the technique and design of the tiles show that they were made by the Tabrizi craftsmen who were in charge of the renovation of the Topkapı Palace between 1526 and 1528.

The same workshop also produced underglaze painted tiles in blue, white, and turquoise and gold leaf stenciled monochrome tiles, which are also preserved on the facades of the circumcision room and the Privy Chamber of the Topkapı Palace. Above all, a group of painted underglaze tiles from the Topkapı Palace deserve special attention. The circumcision room, which was built in 1641, was faced with earlier tile panels that were originally made to decorate a pavilion built by Süleyman in 1527-8 as part of his extensive restoration work in the Topkapı Palace. Five single tiles in long rectangular shapes are perhaps the largest tiles ever attempted in the world (Fig.

Fig. 37 Circumcision room tiles, Topkapı Palace Museum

37 Circumcision room tiles, Topkapı Palace Museum). Each piece measure 125cm in height but the glaze and coloring are flawless. They are painted in blue and turquoise over a white ground. The decoration consists of birds and kylins (mythical Chinese animal), and a vase shown amongst foliage of *saz* leaves and peonies. A narrow arch placed on the very top and decorated with cloud bands complete the design. Four of the five tiles were made from two separate pounced designs to create mirrored images. Due to the mastery in the drawing and the application of the drawings on the flawless tiles, it is highly likely that Şah Kulu himself executed the design, and that the tiles were produced in the court workshops in Istanbul.

We continue seeing the products of the court tile workshop in a few other public buildings, mosques, and mausoleums up to the 1550's. In the early days of the workshop *cuerda seca* tiles were confined to small areas like the window arches or rectangular panels. The colors included blue, turquoise, green, white, yellow, purple, and occasionally overglaze painted brownish red. Symmetrical compositions based on arabesques became more complex and started to be applied on a larger scale in the 1540's. In fact, a building was completely covered with *cuerda seca* tiles in its interiors: the Şehzade Mehmed Tomb was built in 1543-48 for the beloved son of Süleyman, whose death created much sadness to Süleyman and his wife Hürrem. A tomb and mosque complex was built in his name by Süleyman. Architect Sinan was in charge of the buildings and their decoration. The tomb was completely covered with *cuerda seca* tiles of green, blue, turquoise, yellow, purple, and white colors. Interestingly not only the usual repertoire of the *cuerda seca* tiles, that is the peonies and split leafs, but also the serrated *saz* leaves in the Şah Kulu style were incorporated in the design of the tiles. The calligraphic panels reciting sections from the Koran were made part of the tile decoration. The calligraphy was designed most likely by the court calligrapher Ahmed Karahisari.

Although experimented with the Şehzade Mehmed Tomb, the colorful *cuerda seca* technique did not yield a suitable ground for the new *saz* style. The details of this design could be best viewed over a white plain ground like the circumcision room tiles discussed above. Thus eventually underglaze tiles replaced *cuerda seca* tiles in Ottoman architectural decoration. The shift also better harmonized with the white stone and marble revetments of Ottoman buildings. Thus the tile makers switched to the underglaze technique to adopt this new style in their products.

Tile revetments were part of the carefully planned interior and exterior decorations of several monuments that Sinan built. The court workshops were limited and unable to handle the large quantities of tiles necessary for the monuments. Thus by the mid-16th century the tile making industry moved almost completely to Iznik. And once Iznik took over, the number of imperial tile makers decreased in the court workshops. Numerous mosques and tombs in various parts of the Ottoman

Empire, especially in Istanbul, show the extensive output of the Iznik tile production.

Although Iznik tile makers were not salaried court artists, their production of tiles was regulated by the court, and court designs were provided for their use. It appears that the same kilns were used for tiles and ceramics. Thus as tile production increased in Iznik ceramic production decreased, and in the second half of the 16th century the ceramic industry became a part of the tile industry.

Before the 1550's underglaze tiles were blue and white and hexagonal in shape. Under pressure to produce high quality tiles in short periods of time, standardization of tiles in shape and size became necessary in the Iznik production. The square shape, which was better suited to multiunit compositions, became standard. For great pictorial and calligraphic panels stencils were used. The standardization allowed orders from Iznik to be applied without difficulty in distant places. For more specialized areas, like curved surfaces or calligraphic panels, the collaboration of the chief architect with the tile makers must have been more intense. In the 1540's and 50's the underglaze tile work expanded its palette to include green and purple. The purple disappeared soon since it was not visible from a distance. Red, which was introduced in the 1550's, increased visibility. Red was applied over a layer of slip to stop it from running under the glaze. First the slip was applied thinly but then the results were uneven. When the slip was applied liberally then the red became even and rich. This technical requirement also created a slight relief effect on the tiles, which helped visibility. Over time tile makers experimented and achieved a coral tone.

The Süleymaniye Complex was the first of its kind to combine architecture and decorative arts to achieve a high standard of harmony. Tile work, calligraphy, metalwork, wall painting, inlaid woodwork, stained window glass, carpets and illuminated

Korans were produced almost simultaneously by court artists specifically for this monument. The mosque, which was one of Sinan's best works, was finished in 1557. The limited tile decoration of the mosque only hints at the new achievements of the Iznik tile industry. Inside the mosque only the *mihrab* wall is decorated with tiles. This decorative restraint is suggested to be related to the religious strictness that Süleyman gained in his older age. The tile decoration can be seen on both sides of the *mihrab* in two circular calligraphic panels designed by Hasan Karahisari. These circular designs are set in two large squares that consist of several square tiles, which had to be designed individually possibly by the use of pounced paper models. The white letters are set on a dark blue ground and the four corners of the square are designed with minute scrolling arabesques, and medallions with cloud bands predominantly in blue and turquoise over a white ground. Red color, which is a brick tone, is only used as a bordering line. The floral designs in general are too minute to be recognized from a distance. There are also tiled window arches inside as well as outside the mosque facing the courtyard. These also include calligraphic bands bordered with *saz* leaves, and *hatayis*.

The tomb of Hürrem Sultan built in the southern courtyard of the Süleymaniye Mosque in 1559 after Süleyman's beloved wife's death, exemplifies the Iznik tile production in full bloom. This octagonal tomb is fully tiled in its interior up to the beginning of the dome. The tiles include the new repertoire of naturalist flowers in the Kara Memi style, creating a paradise-like space. Unlike the mosque's tile decoration, here calligraphic panels and large floral designs are easily recognizable from a distance. The red is also a nice brilliant tomato red that the Iznik tile makers had newly achieved. Ceramic vases are recorded to have once decorated the tomb.

Fig. 38 Rüstem Pasha Mosque mihrab tiles

A major mosque in Istanbul that utilizes tile decoration to an extreme level was built by Sinan for Rüstem Pasha, the grand vizier and son in law of Süleyman. The building of a large Friday mosque was in Rüstem Pasha's will but the mosque was built by his wife Mihrümah after his death with the funds he reserved for this purpose. A mosque converted from a church previously occupied the land. With permission of the highest religious authority and the sultan, the area was cleared in 1562 and a large mosque was built in the following year by Sinan in a commercial and busy part of Istanbul according to Rüstem's will. The mosque was built on top of a series of warehouses and shops to provide income for the endowment of the mosque. Architecturally these shops allowed the mosque to be higher and also separated from the bustle of commercial activity. The spandrels of columns in the second portico and the entrance to the mosque on the northern façade of the mosque covered with Iznik tiles greet the people to an illusionary garden as they separate themselves from the commercial life below the mosque. These underglaze tiles are decorated with large flowery designs in the Kara Memi style that are legible from a distance. The interior of the mosque (up to the beginning of the arches but also on the curved surfaces above the second tier arches) is completely covered with Iznik tiles (Fig. 38 Rüstem Pasha Mosque *mihrab* tiles). Here Kara Memi's naturalist plants such as tulips, blossoming trees, pomegranates, and carnations coexist with *saz* leaves (Fig. 39 Rüstem Pasha Mosque tiles). As applied on the Süleymaniye Mosque and the tomb of Hürrem, there are also large calligraphic panels with inscriptions from the Koran, sayings of the Prophet Muhammad, and additional prayers in Arabic. The colors range from blue, turquoise, and purple with details of red. The red color on the tiles here fluctuates in hue due to the various skills of the craftsmen from different ateliers. While some tiles were created for specific locations as a single panel design (such as on the entrance panels, of which only one

Fig. 39 Rüstem Pasha Mosque tiles

survives, or the curvy surfaces upon which the dome rests), many more modular tiles were used to cover the large areas on the wall and piers. Perhaps due to the sheer number of required tiles, many different hands are visible in the decoration. This variety points to the efforts of the different ateliers in Iznik, which were culled for the large project to be completed in a short time. Various ateliers must have been provided with court designs. The ogival designs placed on top of vases similar to that on the circumcision room tile in the Topkapı Palace and the undulating vines with *saz* leaves bear a close resemblance to the textile patterns of this period (see below). Not only do these patterns on the tiles mark Rüstem Pasha's commercial interests in the textile and tile industry (Rüstem Pasha had personally accumulated large revenues from both) but also the widely circulating designs of the court studio lead by Şah Kulu until 1556 and Kara Memi afterwards.

The lavish use of tiles in the Rüstem Pasha Mosque was never repeated by Sinan in another mosque. The juxtaposition of this lavishness with the limited use of tiles even in the Sultan's own mosque has been questioned by scholars. Rüstem's large endowment allocated by Rüstem and run by his luxury loving wife after his death was surely used up to the full extent in order to create a befitting mosque for the deceased husband of the princess. Interestingly Mihrümah's own mosque built by herself in Edirnekapı in 1569 utilizes only painted decoration (now replaced by modern ones) despite its architectural connection to the Rüstem Pasha Mosque. The tomb of Rüstem Pasha on the other hand built in 1561 by Mihrümah in the garden of the Şehzade Mosque also utilizes Iznik tiles to a large extent.

Ceramics

Up until the mid-16th century Iznik, Kütahya, and Istanbul were the main ceramic producing centers. The court tile workshops in the Tekfur Sarayı district in Istanbul must have been involved with small-scale ceramic production under

Master Habib's direction in the 1520's. The production in Iznik and Kütahya was most likely continuous from the 15th century without a break. However the appearance of some novel motifs and colors in Ottoman ceramics in the 1520's may have been due to intensified relations between tile and ceramic workshop at the court and provincial ceramic centers. Tiles and ceramics shared similar motifs and techniques as they were made in the same workshops and kilns with a similar repertoire of designs.

The ceramics produced in the early reign of Selim continue the blue and white color scheme. A mosque lamp from the mosque of Selim produced during the early reign of Süleyman represents the small but high quality ceramic production in Istanbul at the court workshops. This lamp's decoration consists of only two bands of calligraphy written in blue over a white ground and the white areas were once fully gilded over the glaze.

The production that followed Selim's conquests included more experimentation in ceramics. Some of the experimentation was in shapes. Chinese porcelains brought in large quantities by Selim from Tabriz and Cairo were imitated by Ottoman potters who produced dishes with foliated rims or rimless deep dishes in blue and white. There were also new shapes like the European tondino ceramics, long flasks perhaps imitating Venetian glass, and cylindrical tankards.

There was also experimentation with colors and designs. Several new designs also began to emerge on new and old ceramic shapes as the court studio and ceramics workshops in the city and provinces interacted.

A spiraling design closely related to illuminations on the sultan's *tuğras* was applied to several ceramics. Most likely initial examples of this type were made in court workshops in Istanbul but soon it was made in provincial centers. A fragmentary water bottle with this spiraling style was made in Kütahya in 1529 (written in Armenian on the bottle itself).

Şah Kulu's *saz* style was also used around the same time on ceramics. One fragmentary dish in Vienna shows how closely Şah Kulu style drawings were applied on ceramics, which must have been produced, and (perhaps solely) in court workshops. As we first see on the circumcision room tiles from 1528 (see fig. 37) turquoise began to be used on blue and white ceramics in 1530's. The color was applied on ceramics first with the *saz* style and spiraling decorations.

Although this shift may seem small, it opened up new experiments with other colors such as manganese purple and olive green, which helped the creation of painterly surfaces on ceramics. By the middle of the century red was also added, first as an orange tone then a bright tomato tone, to the ceramic repertoire as in the tiles. However, purple, which did not have a strong tone, was slowly eliminated.

With the dissemination of naturalist flowers in the Kara Memi style on ceramics, tulips, hyacinths, pomegranates, roses, and artichoke-like trees began to be used as main elements of design usually combined with older style motifs. The Kara Memi style was more easily applied on ceramics then the Baba Nakkaş or Şah Kulu *saz* styles. It also allowed more freedom to the craftsmen. The results were painterly surfaces that often required freehand drawings by the ceramic makers applied under a clear transparent glaze.

But in the 1550's emphasis shifted from ceramics to tiles in the Iznik production. Under the pressure of large tile commissions, possibly due in short time, ceramic makers worked on increasingly standard and less complex shapes in ceramics. Ambitious shapes were abandoned in favor of small-size objects. The details of the designs also moved away from the once-court-designed finesse towards a more relaxed style. However, as we understand from imperial decrees from the second half of the 16th century, patterns prepared by court designers continued to be applied on ceramics made for royal patrons in provincial centers. The court also bought readymade examples available on the market. The workshops in Iznik and Kütahya produced ceramics of differing quality levels for various types of patrons. Perhaps due to this variety their popular appeal never diminished, and today almost all the intact examples of İznik ceramics are in collections outside of Turkey.

Textiles

Luxury fabrics were in high demand at the Ottoman court both in domestic and public ceremonial life. Not only were they made into robes, but also used as decorative hangings, awnings and tents. In the 15th and the early 16th centuries, the Ottoman court used to import high quantities of luxury textiles from Italy, especially Venice. Bursa was a silk waving center in Byzantine times. Under the Ottoman rule the city continued to be a center of silk production. It also served as a center for the international silk trade. The production of silk and its sale were under strict control by the Ottoman state since taxes from both sides were a good source of revenue. Bursa velvets were especially famous in the 15th century.

In the 1540's luxury textiles began to be produced locally at court workshops in Istanbul due to Rüstem Pasha's limitations on imports. The number of court artisans related to their production clearly shows this unprecedented output: the number of artisans increased from 27 in 1526, to 105 in 1545 and 156 in 1557. By the end of Süleyman's reign the textile court workshop of Istanbul had the highest number of workers among the court workshops. The grand vizier Rüstem Pasha, who seems to be behind this shift, supported the local production of silks and velvets for the Ottoman court. Even a cursory look at Ottoman textiles shows that designs of the court studio were incorporated into these textiles in large scale. Specially trained textile designers must have enlarged the small patterns of the court designers in order to apply them into the woven texture of the textiles. Many types of silk and velvet were also decorated with gold or silver (as either brocade applied on the textile or wefts as inherent part of the textiles). Such textiles were in high demand so much so that the court sometimes had to impose bans on the production of such textiles in order to keep enough reserves of gold and silver. While the court production was exempt from such bans, the export of these textiles was strictly controlled.

Parallel with the increase in the number of workmen in the court workshops towards the mid-16th century, the variety of motifs on Ottoman textiles multiplied. As we see on the tiles and ceramics, several motifs from the Şah Kulu style were blended with the new naturalist motifs of Kara Memi. Usually executed in bold colors, which increased visibility even from a distance, several garden flowers, pomegranates, pine cones, crescents, and triple dot and/or wavy lines called *çintemani* (Fig. 40 Velvet caftan, Topkapı Palace Museum, 13/6) began to dominate Ottoman textiles towards the mid-16th century and onwards. A ceremonial silk caftan, which is a long robe with equally long decorative sleeves (Fig. 41 Silk caftan, Topkapı Palace Museum, 13/37), is decorated with *saz* leaves and *hatayis* with fine details of red, white, blue, and green details over a dark green ground. Small blossoming hyacinths are also recognizable. The decoration bears close similarities to the tiles of

Fig. 40 Velvet caftan, Topkapı Palace Museum, 13/6

the period and shows the creative output of the court textile makers and court designers. The robe is cut from a piece of textile on which the motifs are repeated only in the front. Also the robe is cut in the front in such a way that the design continues uninterrupted on the other side. The robe most likely belonged to Şehzade Bayezid, son of Süleyman. An exact design applied on a cream ground was used on another robe, which possibly belonged to another son of Süleyman, Şehzade Mustafa. Both textiles were made of seven different colored silks in a highly difficult technique. It appears that these textiles were designed and produced just to make these specific robes.

Fig. 41 Silk caftan, Topkapı Palace Museum, 13/37

When the sultan or other court officials wore robes made of boldly colored, often brocaded textiles, their effect in crowded public ceremonies would have been inescapable (see fig. 58 below). Brocaded silks would create shiny and colorful surfaces noticed even at a distance, and of course when such robes were worn by several people in a ceremony, their effect would have been even greater. The sultan's and his royal household officers' ceremonial clothes created much awe in foreigners who witnessed such occasions.

Carpets

In the middle of the 16th century a specific type of carpet began to be produced in the Ottoman realm. These carpets of large size were woven of soft wool, cotton, and occasionally silk (used in the warp). A Persian style knotting known as

Senneh was used instead of the traditional Gördes knot, typical for Turkish carpets. (The denser *Senneh* knot permitted easier application of detailed curvy designs). The design usually consists of a central medallion and four corner pieces, but unlike the earlier Uşak carpets, the areas between the medallions are larger and dominated by large serrated leaves and *hatayis* of the

Fig. 42 Court carpet, Istanbul Turkish and Islamic Art Museum, 153

saz style (Fig. 42 Court carpet, Istanbul Turkish and Islamic Art Museum, 153). Tulips, hyacinths, carnations, roses, and spring blossoms are also found in the designs. They have a graphic similarity to the Ottoman textiles of the same period. Whether these carpets were woven in Istanbul, Bursa or Cairo is still argued but it would not be too difficult to assume that their initial production was in Istanbul just like the tiles.

Court workshops, which were established in Istanbul for fine carpet weaving, were probably augmented with the artisans arriving from Tabriz and Cairo after the conquests of Selim I.

The court carpet weavers, who are recorded as being a total of 18 during the reign of Bayezid II (1481-1512), increased in number to 25 by Süleyman's reign according to surviving court documents. By the end of the 16th century their numbers dropped again and finally in the early 17th century the division of court carpet weavers was abolished. These carpet weavers were probably responsible for the new type of carpets produced for the court. The designs of the decoration of new carpets, especially in their combination of *saz* style and Kara Memi flowers, clearly suggest that the court studio provided designs to these carpet workshops. By the second half of the 16th century court carpets were woven also in Cairo following designs specifically created by court artists.

The demand for carpets by the court must have increased as well since Süleyman built large mosques and carpets would have been necessary to furnish them. For example, very large red ground Süleymaniye carpets were specifically woven to harmonize with the entire decoration. However it is not known what types of designs were used on them. Most likely these carpets would have been prayer rugs featuring multiform arches with lamps hanging from them.

Metalwork

Special objects of metalwork, especially those made for the sultan, show the high technical and aesthetic achievements of the court workshops in this area. Several metal objects, including ceremonial armor, or a rare type of bookbinding, were also jeweled. A ceremonial sword most likely prepared for the victorious return of Süleyman from his Mohaç campaign is one of the masterpieces of Ottoman metalwork (Fig. 43 Ceremonial sword, Topkapı Palace Museum, 2/3776). The sword combines ivory, rubies, gold, and steel. The steel blade is inscribed in Arabic with a dedication to Süleyman and the date 1526. The hilt of the sword, which is made of ivory, is decorated with

Fig. 43 Ceremonial sword, Topkapı Palace Museum, 2/3776

a scrolling design in black mastic. It is overlaid with cloud bands and *hatayis* in gold. The blade itself is decorated with an intricate design. A phoenix and a dragon are shown in combat. The decoration continues with an animated scroll. The rubies are used only as highlights on the hilt and on the blade. The design clearly comes out of the Şah Kulu style, and may have been made by him. The spine of the blade gives the name of the artist as Ahmed Tekelü, who may have been one of the craftsmen brought by Selim I from Tabriz.

Ivory

An ivory mirror dated to 1543 and signed by an artist named Gani is one of the masterpieces of ivory work in Ottoman decorative arts (Fig. 44 Mirror, Topkapı Palace Museum, 2/2893). The handle and the backing for the mirror are made of wood. The back of the mirror is made of two ivory pieces attached with golden nails to the backing. The carved decoration is conceived in three levels. The highest central level is decorated with a symmetric scroll design with various *hatayi* and *rumi* motifs. The middle zone repeats the same shape but is decorated with a scroll design made of *hatayis* and cloud bands. The last and lowest level is decorated with a carved inscription over a thin scrolling design. The inscription is a Turkish poem by the maker of the mirror who wishes the longevity of his work and his prayers to be accepted by God. The artist placed his name Gani in the narrow part of the mirror attaching to the handle. The mirror not only shows the skills of the artist in this medium but also the application of the favorite court designs of the period on ivory.

Fig. 44 Mirror, Topkapı Palace Museum, 2/2893

Chapter 5

Impact of court workshops on Ottoman decorative arts: 1566-1595

Historical setting

When Selim II ascended the Ottoman throne at the age of 42 following his father's death in 1566 he had no rivals left in the family due to the efforts of his powerful mother Hürrem. Although he had been a governor in Konya, Manisa and Kütahya before his accession to the throne, Selim II chose not to be involved in government affairs when he became the sultan and left the administration in the hands of his son in law the grand vizier Sokollu Mehmed Pasha. Selim II, unlike his namesake Selim I (1512-1520), never left Istanbul for a campaign during his reign. In fact he was the first Ottoman sultan who did not command the Ottoman army in person. Sokollu Mehmed Pasha led a campaign against Yemen in order to stop an uprising. In the west a treaty was signed with the Austrians in 1568, who agreed to pay an annual sum to the Ottomans. Similar agreements were renewed with the French. In 1570 Cyprus, which was controlled by the Venetians, was conquered by vizier Lala Mustafa Pasha in order to safeguard the eastern Mediterranean trade and travel for hajj pilgrims. Nicosia and Famagusta were conquered in 1570-71. As a response the Venetians gathered a large navy aided by the Pope and the Spanish, and won a victory against the Ottoman navy in Lepanto (at the Golf of Corinth in present day Greece) in 1571. Psychologically this battle had an enormous impact in Europe since a century after the conquest of Constantinople the Ottomans were finally defeated by the European forces. However the truce signed with the Venetians confirmed Ottoman supremacy and forced the Venetians to pay a large war indemnity. The Ottoman navy, which was quickly rebuilt after Lepanto, focused on its struggle with the Spanish and conquered Tunis, which became an Ottoman province along with Algiers and Tripoli. As a result the Spanish decided to focus on its control in the Atlantic and the new world. The geographical extent the Ottomans reached was almost beyond their capacity to control and thus they never attempted to play a role in the Atlantic. Overall during the short reign of Selim II the Ottoman military gains continued, but slowed down.

Selim II was known in the west as the sot for the life style he acquired. Although he had many consorts, he only married his Venetian born chief consort Nurbanu after their son Murad was singled out as the heir in 1571. Selim enjoyed luxury in his lifestyle and clothing. He wore jewels, plumes, and voluminous turbans. Garden outings were famous during his time and lasted several days and nights with feasts including drinking, music, and poetry. He wrote poetry under the penname Selimi and was skilled in archery.

Murad III ascended the throne in 1574 at the age of 28 after being a governor of Manisa for 12 years. Like his father he did not command the army in its campaigns and sent his viziers instead. His reign on the whole was not a major period of military success. An eastern campaign against the Safavids between 1578 and 90 brought Georgia and other Iranian provinces bordering the Caspian Sea under Ottoman control. In the west he made a campaign towards Hungary to defend Ottoman rights against Austrian Habsburg attacks but only minor fortresses were captured.

Murad III's reign was marked with the short offices of the viziers after Sokollu Mehmed Pasha, who had been a grand vizier since the reign of Süleyman, was killed. The queen mother Nurbanu Sultan, who used the title sultan officially for the first time, and Murad's sister Ismihan Sultan had increasing influence on Murad and palace life. Despite high inflation, bribery, military rebellions, and administrative problems, which affected daily life in Istanbul, festivities, performances, and palace protocol became very important during Murad III's reign. The black eunuchs became responsible for the harem for the first time instead of the white ones. Since Murad III received a good education in religion, politics, literature, music and languages as a prince in the Manisa palace he became a generous patron of arts and literature during his reign. He composed poetry with the penname Muradi and wrote separate collections of Persian, Turkish and Arabic poems. He had his first son and successor Mehmed from his chief consort Safiye Sultan but he never married her. When Murad died in 1595 at the age of 49 after reigning for 21 years he had left 49 children from various consorts who were presented to him by his mother and sister.

Architectural activity

Architecturally Selim's short reign of eight years was still dominated by the chief architect Sinan's works. After his father's death, Selim built a tomb for Süleyman in the southern courtyard of his father's Süleymaniye Mosque. His major architectural activity was his own mosque complex Selimiye built in Edirne between 1568 and 1574. The complex which coincided with the Cyprus victory in 1570 consists of a mosque, *medrese*, religious school, timekeeper's room, and a series of shops (although added after Sinan died they too may have been conceived by Sinan). The Selimiye Mosque is considered the zenith of Sinan's architectural genius. Sinan was in his eighties when he built it. The mosque has a commanding dome that rests on an octagonal support system. A very large and uninterrupted central space is achieved under a single dome. An inner fountain and a chanter's (*müezzin*) tribune placed in the middle of this space emphasize its centrality. On the outside the eight weight turrets with pointed lead caps arranged around the dome and the four slender minarets arranged close to the dome visually increase the height of the dome. As we shall see below, its rich decorative program differs considerably from that of Süleymaniye. Selim died before he saw the full completion of his mosque. During Selim's reign Sinan also renovated Hagia Sophia with four minarets. Other planned additions were not completed when Selim died but the addition of Selim's imperial tomb built by his son Murad III turned Hagia Sophia into a funerary mosque of the sultan. Selim also built a large mosque in Konya next to the revered Mevlana Tomb and Shrine. Selim's wife Nurbanu Sultan, his sister, viziers, and admirals also built mosque complexes in Istanbul. The grand vizier Sokollu Mehmed Pasha built mosque complexes including caravansaries in Lüleburgaz and Payas on important trade routes and halting points for the Ottoman army in its military campaigns.

When Selim II died Murad III built a tomb designed by Sinan for his father, who was buried in the courtyard of Hagia Sophia. The tomb was completed in 1577. After a fire in the Topkapı Palace Sinan rebuilt the kitchens in 1574. Unsatisfied with the architecture of the harem in the palace Murad III had new quarters built for his mother Nurbanu and other consorts. Sinan also completed an elegant two-floor pavilion overlooking a large pool in the Topkapı Palace for Murad III in 1579 (known as Murad III's bedroom).

The public architectural activity sponsored by Murad III was mainly outside of Istanbul. He completed additions to the Kaaba in Mecca begun by his father. He remodeled the Prophet's mosque in Medina and built there a *medrese*, hospice, an elementary school, and a convent functioning as a guesthouse for the dervishes and the poor. His building activity included a few other dervish convents or additions to them in Medina, Kars, and Konya. He also commissioned a large mosque in Manisa designed by Sinan but executed by royal architects between 1583 and 1586. Interestingly the sultan did not leave Istanbul to see his completed mosque in Manisa. Sinan built several mosques for Murad's mother, viziers, and important statesmen in Istanbul and elsewhere. Important mosque-caravanserai complexes continued to be built on important trade routes by Murad's viziers. After Sinan's death in 1588 architectural activity slowed down somewhat. Sinan's student architect Davut Ağa became the chief architect.

Decorative arts

The reigns of Selim II and Murad III were perhaps the zenith of Ottoman decorative arts. The variety and artistic creativity achieved in the 1550's during Süleyman's reign continued with more lavish and ostentatious works during this period. The highest number of artists at the court workshops was reached during this time. A court document dated to 1596 lists 129 salaried artists in the court studio (*nakkaşhane*) alone. The activity in the semi autonomous workshops in the provinces also supplemented the needs of the Ottoman court. Decorated manuscripts, tiles, ceramics, textiles, metalwork, and woodwork all show the full impact of the court workshops and the rich resources available to the artists of the Ottoman court who received patronage from the Ottoman sultan and his close entourage.

Decorated manusripts

The periods of Selim II and Murad III were the most prolific in terms of Ottoman decorated manuscripts, especially illustrated ones produced for the Ottoman court. The number of illustrated manuscripts reached 50 and included hundreds of miniatures.

During the reign of Selim II (1566-74), the author Lokman became the court's official history writer (*şehnameci*) in the Persian literary style of the *Şahname* (see previous chapter). Lokman worked with a number of scribes and painters (*nakkaş*) to produce the illustrated Ottoman histories of the period. This team produced several illustrated manuscripts eulogizing the sultans' military activities, especially between 1579 and 1590 during the reign of Murad III, who is considered the most active patron for decorated manuscripts among all Ottoman sultans. The painter Nakkaş Osman was the leader of Lokman's team. According to surviving court records Nakkaş Osman, who most likely joined the court studio between 1559 and 1565, was already a master in 1566 during the reign of Süleyman. Lokman and Nakkaş Osman began working with the orders of the grand vizier Sokollu Mehmed Pasha.

An example of Nakkaş Osman's early work about the military campaign of Süleyman to Hungary and proceeding events is *Nushet el-esrar el-ahbar der sefer- i Sigetvar*. (Chronicle of the Szigetvar campaign). The text written in 1552 in Turkish by Ahmed Feridun relates the events that took place in the last two years of Süleyman's reign, including the military campaign, Süleyman's death, and the accession of Selim II to the Ottoman throne. The illustrated copy was completed in 1569 with twenty miniatures. Almost all of the miniatures display no decorative elements. Osman's portrait-like depictions of Süleyman, Selim II, and Sokollu Mehmed Pasha, and the correctly rendered castle of Szigetvar are remarkable and show the new direction of Ottoman manuscript illustration. A double-page miniature from the manuscript illustrates the long journey Selim II and his retinue made from Manisa where Selim learned of his father's death. (Fig. 45 *Nushet el-esrar el-ahbar der sefer- i Sigetvar*

Fig. 45 Nushet el-esrar el-ahbar der sefer- i Sigetvar Topkapı Palace Museum, H.1339, 83b-84a

Topkapı Palace Museum, H.1339, 83b-84a). In the meantime the death of Süleyman was kept a secret from the Ottoman army by the grand vizier Sokollu Mehmed Pasha until Selim arrived. In the double-page miniature Selim and his men are shown in a sad state. The weariness of the horses and the infantry from the long journey is successfully depicted in the painting. The realistic aspects of this and other miniatures in the manuscript are unprecedented in Islamic manuscript painting. Due to this realism scholars have suggested that Nakkaş Osman was a witness to these events just like Ahmed Feridun, the author of the work.

Examples of Persian and Turkish historical works in which Nakkaş Osman was involved as a head painter of the court studio are numerous:

1) *Zafername* (Book of victories) prepared by Lokman in Persian as *Süleymanname*'s (see previous chapter) last volume was copied in 1579 and illustrated with 25 miniatures. This manuscript is in Dublin now.

2) *Kıyafetü'l İnsaniye fişema'ilü'losmaniye* (Human physiognomy concerning the personal dispositions of the Ottomans) differs somewhat in subject from other historical works and

describes the physical and mental characteristics of the Ottoman sultans including Murad III. It was written by Lokman and illustrated by Nakkaş Osman in 1579 with the portraits of the sultans.

3) *Şahname-i Selimhan* (Epic history of Selim II) written by Lokman in Persian about the events of the reign of Selim II was illustrated with 44 miniatures and completed in 1581.

4) *Şehinşahname* (Book of the king of kings) relates in Persian the events of Murad III's ascension to the throne and the proceeding events until 1579. It was written by Lokman and illustrated in 1581. A second volume was copied in 1592.

5) *Zübdetü't tevarih* (Quintessence of histories) completed by Lokman from an unfinished Turkish manuscript of a previous *Şehname* writer was illustrated with 40 miniatures in 1583. The manuscript begins with the creation of man, continues with the history of the prophets, and concludes with the history of the Ottomans.

6) *Hünername* (Book of achievements) mostly written by Lokman as a narrative also after an unfinished Turkish work was illustrated with 45 miniatures and completed in 1585. It was followed by a second volume in 1588. Like the *Zübdetü't tevarih* it includes the portraits of the sultans. In order to execute the portraits of the 12 Ottoman sultans accurately it is known that information and pictures were sought even from Venetian authorities. This shows how keen the Ottoman painters and historians were in this regard. For example Murad III is the only Ottoman sultan shown with a book in his hand, surely as a result of his patronage of decorated manuscripts.

7) *Surname-i Hümayun* (Imperial Festival Book) written in Turkish by the court scribe İntizami describes the circumcision festival arranged for Şehzade Mehmed, which began on May 14, 1582 and lasted fifty-two days and nights. It was the most luxurious festival up to that date and continued much longer

than previous festivities. In the text the author İntizami mentions that he prepared his manuscript in consultation with Mehmed Ağa and the dwarf Zeyrek Ağa who held high offices at Murad III's court. After Murad's approval of the text an illustrated copy was prepared. This illustrated copy with 250 double-page miniatures was completed in 1588 by a large team that consisted of scribes, binders, painters, and illuminators (*nakkaşan*). It appears that the manuscript was read so many times probably even many years after its composition. Some pages are lost and the original binding has been replaced. According to the information in the manuscript, the miniatures were executed by Nakkaş Osman and his team. İntizami eulogizes the skill of Osman and the high quality of his work. From the text we also learn that Nakkaş Osman had a workshop (probably the court studio adjacent to the *Arslanhane*, see chapter 3) and worked on miniatures, ink drawings, as well as brushwork on walls.

Although executed by different hands most of the miniatures follow the same framework that must have been designed by Nakkaş Osman. While sultan Murad and his son are seated in the elevated balcony of the İbrahim Pasha (vizier and son in law of Süleyman) palace (where the Turkish and Islamic Art Museum is now located, next to the former hippodrome called *At Meydanı* in Turkish) performers or artisans approach them through the crowds, and after performing and presenting their gifts, make a loop around the Column of Constantine (*Burmalı sütun*) and leave the scene. With this basic scheme all the festivities are shown in detail almost like cinematography. In fact this framework became a model for future miniatures illustrating similar festivities. Among the festivities in addition to the performers of music, dance, and acrobatics all the guilds in the city showed their arts and crafts or skills. For example stonemasons carried a model of the Süleymaniye Mosque. Brocaded silk makers passed with the textiles they wove.

Musicians passed while performing music. Pastry, coffee, bread, and kebab makers also passed on mobile kitchens while making their products. These provide documentary evidence for the richness of the arts and crafts during the reign of Murad III. For example glassmakers (Fig. 46 *Surname-i Hümayun*, Topkapı Palace Museum, H. 1344, 32b-33a) show how they were working with glass on a mobile workshop as well as their finished products. In their hands they hold long vases with twisted-necked, hourglasses, bottles, decorated bluish ewers, and vases with lids, which have not otherwise survived from the 16th century. The event is also watched from the top by a crowded group of high Ottoman officials and foreigners (damaged area), who were given special temporary places to watch the festivities. The crowd on the right also consists of high Ottoman officials based on their clothes and large turbans. 8) *Hünername*'s second volume was completed and presented to Murad III in 1589. This copy also illustrated the important achievements of Süleyman.

The court illuminators and calligraphers of this period worked on the largest and perhaps the most important Ottoman Koran of all times. The Koran measures 62x43cm and was

Fig. 46 Surname-i Hümayun, Topkapı Palace Museum, H. 1344, 32b-33a

completed in 12 years between 1584-96 under the patronage of Murad III. Although it is not signed, this copy of the Koran was most likely begun by Ahmed Karahisari during 1545-55, and completed by his student Hasan Karahisari. Among the 300 folios (=600 pages) the first 220 are attributed to the hand of Ahmed Karahisari and the remaining to Hasan Karahisari. Each page is given a full margin from a separate piece of paper (*vassale*). The manuscript is richly illuminated. There is an endowment notation and an illuminated roundel before the actual text of the Koran.

The first verse (*sura*) and the beginning of the second verse of the Koran are copied in two different calligraphic scripts (*muhakkak* and *reyhani*), and arranged as facing pages with rich illumination (Fig. 47 Koran, Topkapı Palace Museum, HS 5, 4a). These are followed by two more illuminated text pages of different arrangements, which feature Ahmed Karahisari's inventive writings. After this, each page is arranged in the same calligraphic scheme: one line of *muhakkak*, five lines of *nesih*, one line of *sülüs*, five more lines of *nesih* and one more line of *muhakkak*. There are 112 illuminated headings

Fig. 47 Koran, Topkapı Palace Museum, HS 5, 4a

and 2360 illuminated rectangle panels (*koltuk*) arranged on both sides of the text on each page. Nakkaş Hasan must have been the main illuminator as he was the head of the court studio at that time. Available court documents indicate that five more illuminators worked on the manuscript. The illuminations vary considerably. Sometimes they repeat each other on the same page but in general there is a wide range of designs with 500 different versions from over 100 compositions. All motifs of the Ottoman decorative repertoire are used but in general the illuminations are not typical. The *saz* style and the Kara Memi floral style decorations are used together, and the motifs of both styles have been magnified. This enlargement, which occasionally makes the motifs unrecognizable, may have been the result of an attempt to harmonize the illuminations with the large scripts on the page.

The leather binding of the manuscript is also a work of art. Court records indicate that Süleyman bin Mehmed, who was the head binder of the court studio, was responsible for the binding with the assistance of two of his students. The black binding is decorated with a central medallion, four corner pieces, and a large surrounding frame. All these areas are gilded and decorated in the *saz* style with cloud bands.

The palace account books provide information on materials bought for the manuscript and other expenses. The order of the purchased materials also gives an idea on how the decorative process was completed. For example, the 'good quality' lapis (which creates the blue color) was bought for the frontispiece, which was executed in one of the last steps of the production of the manuscript. Also liquid gold was purchased for the marginal decorations of the end piece as a last expense. From this we deduce that the illumination at the beginning and the end of the manuscript was created as one of the last parts of the production process of the manuscript. We also learn that a temporary workshop was constructed by court carpenters in the palace for the execution of this manuscript. The same records indicate that the margins, rulings, illumination, and binding were made between 1584 and 1596 under the patronage of Murad III. Unfortunately, when Murad III died he could not see the completion of this work.

Another example of high quality workmanship in calligraphy, illumination, and binding was Murad's own *divan* (collection of poetry) dated to 1588. Murad, who wrote with the penname Muradi, wrote on religious and mystic themes perhaps as a result of his formal education, although his personal lifestyle may have been quite different. The binding carries the date 1588 and is an exquisite work of metalwork and jewelry (Fig. 48 Murad III's *Divan*, Topkapı Palace Museum, outer binding, 2/2107). The outer covers and the flap are made of gold and repeat the usual form of leather book bindings: a central medallion and four corner pieces are the main elements while two borders surround the entire cover. These areas are decorated with encrusted rubies, emeralds, and diamonds over a scrollwork executed in relief on the metal. The remaining field is executed in filigree split leaf (*rumi*) decoration to reveal the blue color of the silk fabric underneath. The inscriptional border written by a poet explains the subject of the poems

Fig. 48 Murad III's Divan, Topkapı Palace Museum, outer binding, 2/2107

in the book and mentions that Zeyrek Ağa was the one who had the book copied and bound for Murad III and that the chief jeweler at the court, Mehmed Bosnavi (of Bosnia) executed the covers in 1588. Mehmed Bosnavi produced many other ceremonial objects encrusted with jewels. Many of these are considered as the classical examples of Ottoman metalwork. Zeyrek Ağa was a dwarf in the entourage of the black Eunuch, who was made more powerful during Murad's reign by being given the charge of the sultan's revenues. Obviously Zeyrek Ağa, who did not spare any expenses for the production of the book, must have conceived it as a gift to the sultan. The jeweler Mehmed Bosnavi (died. c. 1600) is also known from other works he produced for Murad III at the Ottoman court. The gold mounts with precious stones and thc gold chain usc on the spine (back) of the *Divan* binding show his characteristic features skillfully applied on a binding.

Another exquisite binding, which belongs to the *Nusretname*, a history manuscript copied in 1584, represents another example of the use of a different material on a binding (Fig. 49 *Nusretname*, Topkapı Palace Museum, H.1365 outer binding). Fabric bindings were used more occasionally on Ottoman manuscripts during the reign of Mehmed II (1451-

Fig. 49 Nusretname, Topkapı Palace Museum, H.1365 outer binding

1481). However those textiles were not specifically made for the bindings. Thus the decoration of the textile itself was used as a decorative element. In this binding the decoration is specifically embroidered for the binding. A deep red colored silk textile called *atlas* is embroidered with blue, pink, and brown colored silk, silver, and gold threads. The main decoration with a central medallion and four corner pieces repeats that of the leather bindings of the period. While the central medallion repeats *hatayis* (peonies) and *rumis* (split leaves) the corner pieces are decorated with hyacinths of the Kara Memi style. The remaining field is decorated with a dense scroll decoration supplemented with cloud bands and *hatayis*. The spine of the binding is decorated with the *çintemani* (triple dot and wavy lines) motif. The combination of the *saz* and floral style of Kara Memi, and the use of the *çintemani* motif on the same binding show the virtuosity of the embroiderer/cloth binder. The red color embroidered with gold and only highlighted with blue, pink, and brown creates an ostentatious appearance for the binding.

Architectural decoration

The Ottoman tile production that began to accelerate in the 1550's during the reign of Süleyman continued with full force until 1585. During the reign of Selim II and the first decade of Murad III's reign, several large architectural projects conducted by Sinan were lavishly decorated with Iznik tiles. As we shall see, Sinan used tiles to augment the reception of space for a planned program of architecture and meaning. After 1585 we start seeing some problems with such large-scale productions, which lead to the full decline in Iznik production in the following century.

The mausoleum of Süleyman, which was built by Selim II between 1566 and 1568 in the southern courtyard of the Süleymaniye Mosque, was covered to a large extent with

Fig. 50 Tomb of Süleyman

Iznik tiles (Fig. 50 Tomb of Süleyman). However, the general appearance was different from the garden-inspired decoration of the tomb of Hürrem, which was built almost 10 years earlier in 1558. Here a more abstract style was preferred. A large calligraphic band written in white over a blue ground surrounds the interior walls of the octagonal tomb of Süleyman. The other tile revetment below this large band around the windows and also on the pendentives of the main dome feature abstract floral designs. The painted dome is studded with rock crystals and gems.

The Selimiye Mosque complex, built by Sinan in Edirne between 1568 and 1574, was the largest architectural patronage of Selim II during his short reign. On Selim's own request the mosque was lavishly decorated (Fig. 51 Edirne Selimiye mosque, interior). The decoration included Iznik tiles and

Fig. 51 Edirne Selimiye Mosque, interior

brushwork decoration on wood and plaster. The calligraphy on the tiles and the plaster was designed by the famous calligrapher of the period Hasan Karahisari. A large calligraphic band of white letters on a blue ground with verses from the Koran is placed on both sides of the *mihrab*. Large vertical panels with oval medallions in the center and *saz* leaves and *hatayi* flowers around them are placed under an illusionistic arch beneath the calligraphic band. The background is white. Rich colors, including emerald green, red and dark blue are seen on the flowers (Fig. 52 Edirne Selimiye mosque tiles). Other panels with blossoming branches and naturalistic flowers or panels with more repetitive patterns are legible even from a distance. Such panels were made based on pounced paper cartoons created in court studios and then handed over to the tile makers in Iznik. The mosque was planned with a royal tribune just for Selim II on the southeastern corner (left corner of the *mihrab*

Fig. 52 Edirne Selimiye Mosque tiles

wall) of the mosque. This section, which gave Selim seclusion from the main prayer hall, also had a private area with a *mihrab*. It is also covered with Iznik tiles with blossoms and naturalistic flowers featuring a theme of paradise. The inscriptions on the calligraphic panels also reinforce the same theme of Selim's wish to enter paradise. The Iznik panels with blossoming trees were placed at a high level so that everyone in the mosque could see them, even though the sultan himself would not have been seen sitting on the floor behind the wooden lattices.

The painted decorations of the mosque were executed in 1573 by five Greek painters from the Aegean island Chios.

Although the original decoration is preserved, it has been largely reworked in the 19th and 20th centuries (Fig. 53 Edirne Selimiye Mosque brushwork decorations after restoration). The decorative repertoire shows a close similarity to the tiles of the mosque. The painted decoration on the chanter's tribune (*müezzin mahfili*) at the center of the mosque was recovered during a recent restoration project and shows the originality of the painted decoration (See fig. 51). One border includes *saz* leaves and *hatayi* flowers on a red background. Another border is decorated with large ribbon-like cloud bands and *hatayi* flowers painted on a green ground. The rich and harmonious decorations of the Selimiye Mosque are not only excellent works of art displaying the high technical and aesthetic merits of Ottoman decorative arts of the period but also Sinan's ability to design and coordinate all parts of the decoration in respect to his patron Selim's wishes.

Fig. 53 Edirne Selimiye Mosque brushwork decorations after restoration

Another mosque built by Sinan for Sokollu Mehmed Pasha as a gift to his wife in Istanbul is another example of the peak performance of the Iznik tile makers. Sokollu Mehmed Pasha who had become a grand vizier in the last year of Süleyman's reign, served Selim II (and later Murad III) and married Selim's daughter Ismihan Sultan. Sokollu was a Serbian recruit from Bosnia and rose to power during the reign of Selim. He enjoyed an unparalleled authority during Selim's reign, who was inclined to leave all government affairs to him. The mosque at Kadırgalimanı (port of galleys) was built as part of a complex between 1569 and 1571. The mosque was covered with Iznik tiles to a large extent in the *mihrab* wall, pendentives and the window arches inside the mosque. On the outside we see Iznik tiles on window arches on both sides of the entrance of the mosque in the courtyard.

In comparison to the interiors of the Rüstem Pasha Mosque, here the tiled decoration is formed not by repetitive patterns but specifically created designs best seen on the *mihrab* wall. The designs also show a better harmony with the structure of the mosque. The *mihrab* wall is completely covered with tiles including the large windows underneath the arch of the main dome (Fig. 54 Sokollu Mehmed Pasha mosque, *mihrab* wall). The space is organized with calligraphic panels of horizontal and square shapes. The calligraphy is written in white on a blue ground. The areas around the calligraphic designs are divided

Fig. 54 Sokollu Mehmed Pasha Mosque, mihrab wall

into large panels of floral designs. Like in the Selimiye Mosque tiles we see the red and the green colors successfully applied on a white ground under a shiny transparent glaze. The motifs include the *hatayis* and *saz* leaves in an abstract manner. The tiled areas above the molding on the *mihrab* niche are decorated with large size naturalistic flowers of tulips, roses, carnations, and hyacinths, which are legible from a distance. They appear to sprout from the same branch that is seen at the bottom of the panels. The *mimbar* (elevated preaching platform) next to the *mihrab* niche is also tiled on its pyramidal roof and base. It follows the abstract style of decoration of the tiled area on the nearby wall. While the base of the *mimbar* is decorated with *rumi* decorations of small scale similar to book illuminations, the roof is decorated with large-scale *hatayis*.

The six pendentives of the mosque are identically decorated with square tiles. Here the main decoration is the round calligraphic medallions in the center and the large *saz* leaves and *hatayis* legible even from a distance. The rectangular windows all around the interior of the mosque are also capped with tiled panels with calligraphic inscriptions.

The painted decoration of the Sokullu Mehmed Pasha Mosque, now only preserved in small areas in the lateral gallery and the vestibule, shows that a motif repertoire similar to the tiles (*hatayis* and *rumis*) was used with preference for a red background. We also see bookbinding-style designs with a central medallion in the center and four corner pieces in small areas of this painted decoration. It is recorded that some of the 29 carpets of the mosque, which were endowed by Ismihan herself, had similar designs with *mihrab* niches.

The tomb of Selim II in the courtyard of Hagia Sophia was designed by Sinan in 1574 and completed in 1577 during the reign of Murad III. Like his father's tomb Selim II Tomb has a large tiled calligraphic band surrounding the inner walls of the tomb. The areas below the band are also revetted with Iznik tiles.

The decorations in the Topkapı Palace in the suite of rooms built for Murad III still preserve some of the original tile decorations. The main room where the sultan slept is completely decorated with Iznik tiles up to the springing of the dome. A large blue and white calligraphic band reciting the 'Throne' verse from the Koran surrounds the room above the level of the lower windows. Repeating tiles decorated with *rumis* with red backgrounds are used as border tiles to this large band and elsewhere as a delineating element. The larger wall panels are also decorated with repeat tiles of *saz* leaves and *hatayi* flowers on a white background. The main bronze fireplace is framed by beautiful Iznik tiles, which display an illusionistic arch with blooming trees visible through it. The use of Kara Memi style flowers on a blue ground placed under an arch suggests a garden-paradise theme. More tiled panels with blooming trees seen through illusionistic arches, which are now used on the vestibule, must have once covered the facade of the hall. These are decorated in the middle with stylized oval patterns made of large *hatayis* and *rumis* reminiscent of textile designs.

A new royal bath was also built by Murad III in the Topkapı Palace in 1583-85. The bath was planned to be decorated with Iznik tiles as well. We learn from the royal decrees sent to Iznik tile manufacturers that when the order for the baths was not quickly fulfilled, the court forbade the tile makers from working on other projects.

The Muradiye Mosque built by Murad III in Manisa between 1583 and 1586, although a small mosque for the sultan, was also lavishly decorated with calligraphic Iznik tiles, especially in the *mihrab* wall arranged like a large niche itself.

After 1585 there was not much court patronage for tile production during the reign of Murad III. The number and size of court commissions fell with the overall decrease in architectural activity. There was a slight technical decline and the draftsmanship suffered as well. A duller green and a less orange-red began to be made. Tile examples from the Takkeci İbrahim Ağa Mosque in Istanbul dated to 1591 signal these features although a luxurious level is achieved overall. The problem seems to be related to the payments of the court. Towards the end of the 16th century the inflation of the Ottoman silver coin with the influx of silver from the New World caused an unprecedented increase in the cost of materials and also the transportation of the tiles. However, prices were set by the state in such a way (a square tile was a fixed rate) that the craftsmen made almost no profit in their large tile productions for the imperial projects. This resulted in the lowering of the quality from the technical and also artistic point of view. The tile manufacturers also began to supplement their income by resorting to ceramic production since ceramic prices were not regulated by the state and could be sold at a profitable rate in the open market. When the tile makers sold ceramics to merchants, who would then sell them to the populace and foreigners, the court started to have difficulties with their orders and occasionally reverted to forced limitation on outside orders. But the decline in tile production also eventually affected the ceramic production as well.

Ceramics

During the reigns of Selim II and Murad III, we start seeing new motifs such as cypresses, boats, and animal figures, and more of the combination of Kara Memi flowers on Ottoman ceramics made in Iznik and Kütahya. Technically creations of the Süleyman era continued, especially after the 1550's: red was abundantly used in addition to purple, blue, green, and white colors. A coating of finely ground quartz slip provided a brilliant white ground. A mosque lamp from the Sokollu Mehmed Pasha Mosque completed in 1571 shows the use of red, dark blue, and turquoise with the white of the ground of the slip on the same vessel (Fig. 55 Mosque lamp, Istanbul Archaeological Museum, Çinili Köşk, 41/17). The shape and size of the lamp repeat those made for the Süleymaniye Mosque. The large bosses on the lamp are considered to resemble those on metal mosque lamps. The decoration consists of a calligraphic band on the neck and a floral arrangement on the body. Beyond the large *hatayis* almost free hand branches ending with *saz* leaves exemplify the use of the abstract floral style with the Kara Memi inspired naturalism on the same surface. The dark blue color is, however, somewhat less skillfully applied as one can see various shades as traces of its application.

Fig. 55 Mosque lamp, Istanbul Archaeological Museum, Çinili Köşk, 41/17

Various Iznik ceramics show that the same patterns were also applied on tiles and ceramics. Ceramic makers were freer to apply the patterns on more decorative grounds like the fish scale motif. With the introduction of slip wares color began to be used on ceramics as a background or just by itself. Slip colors such as salmon pink, pinky beige, or a chocolate brown were applied on several ceramics mostly in the 1570's and 1580's. A group of vase-shaped bottles from the Selimiye Mosque in Edirne were made in the decorated and plain slip technique around 1575.

Blue and white colored ceramics continued but they were modeled less on Chinese decorations. In a way, they were popular versions of the earlier court designs of the Baba Nakkaş style of the reign of Mehmed II and Bayezid II (see chapter 3). Towards the end of Murad III's reign, eclectic combinations of earlier motifs with the new ones became more apparent. A new idea was to introduce figures. Animals, ships and to a small extent people began to be used as decoration. Birds, mostly peacocks, were frequently shown amidst trees. European coats of arms on some dishes show that orders were made specifically for European clientele as well. Several Iznik ceramics that have received European additions indicate the widespread European interest in Iznik ceramics that began in the late 16th century.

Court records indicate that 492 Iznik dishes were removed from the palace and 541 new ones were bought for the banquets during the circumcision festival of Murad III's sons in 1582 (discussed above). Interestingly the Topkapı Palace collections of Iznik ceramics are meager despite the large collections of Far eastern ceramics. Large fires, which damaged the palace kitchens more than once, are thought to be the reason for the lack of Iznik ceramics, which were used as daily wares in the palace. European collections on the other hand display all the variant Iznik ceramics, which were exported from Iznik in high quantities in the 16th century.

Textiles

Luxurious textiles made of silk (*kemha*, *seraser,* and velvet) continued to be made during the reigns of Selim II and Murad III. We learn that in 1577, 268 looms were working in Istanbul and 88 of them worked just for the court. The number of court weavers remained more or less around 156 until the end of the 16th century. They were responsible for producing brocaded silk textiles that specifically used gold and silver threads, which create a shimmering effect even from a distance. Clothes made of these textiles were especially important for court ceremonies where the glittering would match the ostentatious image of the sultan and his entourage. A court record dated to 1568 indicates that 103 bolts of silk textiles (*seraser*, *kemha* and velvet) were produced in one month and more were bought from the market.

Occasionally just like on Iznik productions, some limitations were imposed or at least tried to be imposed on the textile producers outside the court. For example, Selim II tried to decrease their number in relation to the court weavers to keep the production of certain high-end luxury textiles as a monopoly of the court. Yet, we see that the court often resorted to textiles produced outside the court since the need for robes as gifts (*hilat*) multiplied even more with the increasing number of offices in the Ottoman administrative system. For example, vizier Mehmed Pasha was given 30 types or bolts of brocaded silk (*seraser*) textiles as gifts from the sultan after the 1582 circumcision festival of Şehzade Mehmed. After the 1580's court orders had difficulty even to be fulfilled since the court's low tariffs were an impediment against the stronger market values. The same low tariffs were also a problem for the tiles as we have seen above.

Dated Ottoman tiles, dated *tuğras,* and dated decorated manuscripts are helpful in determining the types, patterns, and uses of Ottoman textiles within the 16th century. It appears that the decorative repertoire on textiles of this period continued Kara Memi's flower style with combinations of the *hatayis* and *rumis* of the *saz* style. This style, which first became apparent on the textiles around 1560, forms the basis of typical Ottoman textiles for the reign of Selim II and Murad III (in fact also throughout the next century). Among the miniatures of the *Surname* illustrating the 1582 festival of the Şehzade Mehmed mentioned above, are shown guilds, which produced a type of brocaded silk (*kemha*). In this painting we see small and large patterned *çintemanis* (triple dot and wavy line), large *rumis*, medallions with *hatayis*, and medallions with tulips on the textiles. While these motifs are not unique to the reigns of Selim II and Murad III, the fineness of the details on the patterns and variety in the application of these patterns become more apparent. A comparison with the tiles of the period shows that court designs were applied in both mediums. A brocaded velvet from the second half of the 16th century shows an interesting use of the white crescent on a violet ground detailed in blue (Fig. 56 Brocaded velvet, Konya Mevlana Museum, 616). This cloth was most likely prepared as a tomb cover as it was a custom to place valuable textiles on the tombs of revered people. Velvets appear to have been mostly woven in Bursa although brocaded velvets were woven in court workshops in Bursa for a while in the second half of the 16th century.

Fig. 56 Brocaded velvet, Konya Mevlana Museum, 616

Many collections in Europe and Russia are rich with Ottoman textiles since they were also used as gifts by the Ottoman sultan for the ambassadors. These valuable textiles were also used for church vestments. Therefore many Russian churches have rich collections of robes made of Ottoman textiles. Beyond the usual use of textiles as robes, valuable brocaded textiles were also used to spread to the feet of the sultan or his horse if he was mounted in court ceremonies. A miniature from a later manuscript (see fig. 58) shows that luxury textiles were used to blockade the crowds placed on both sides of the sultan in a procession.

Woodwork

The wooden doors of Murad III's pavilion in the Topkapı Palace, which was built by Sinan between 1578 and 1579, is a good example of the typical Ottoman woodwork inlayed with materials like mother of pearl or ivory (Fig. 57 Doors of the pavilion of Murad III, Topkapı Palace Museum, 8/1077). The doors are decorated with a symmetrical geometric decoration. Each shutter has a long middle panel with two narrow ones above and below it. There are further borders and cartouches around the main panels. The middle and lower panels are decorated with a design that generates from a ten-pointed star. This star scheme was widely used on doors from the Seljuk period (11th - 13th centuries) onwards. However, here the flat surfaces created by the lines are inlaid with mother of pearl, tortoise shell, ebony, and ivory. The top panels are decorated with the same materials with a calligraphic inscription in the *sülüs* script. These inscriptions mention a pavilion that may refer to the one mentioned in the Koran or the legendary eight pavilions best known from the Persian literary classics. Since Sinan's mosques and tombs often have specific inscriptional programs that augment the general meaning of the monument for a specific patron one can easily see a similar reference between Murad's pavilion and those mentioned above. In fact, since Sinan was first trained in woodwork it is suggested that these doors are his own work. We know that Sinan's student and follower, the architect Mehmed Ağa, learned the art of inlaid woodwork as well as architecture from Sinan. We know that with the encouragement of Sinan, Mehmed Ağa excelled in woodwork and later presented several inlaid wooden works to Murad III in the 1590's. These and other inlayed works gave Mehmed Ağa the cognomen *sedefkar* (mother of pearl inlayer). It is likely that Mehmed Ağa assisted Sinan on these specific doors.

Fig. 57 Doors of the pavilion of Murad III, Topkapı Palace Museum, 8/1077

Chapter 6

Variations on Classical styles: 1595-1703

Historical setting

The 17th century was historically a period of continuity albeit a less opulent one for the Ottoman Empire. Ten Ottoman sultans reigned over a hundred years and most of the sultans reigned less then a decade: Mehmed III (1595-1603), Ahmed I (1603-1617), Mustafa I (1617-18), Osman II (1618-22), Mustafa I for a second time (1622-23), Murad IV (1623-40), İbrahim I (1640-48), Mehmed IV (1648-87), Süleyman II (1687-91), Ahmed II (1691-95), and Mustafa II (1695-1703). Only the reigns of Ahmed I, Murad IV, and, in particular Mehmed IV, were long compared to the others.

Military successes were limited especially compared to the previous centuries. The campaigns against Austria in 1596 and Iran in 1603-4 showed that further military expansion was impossible. Only in 1645-69 was Crete conquered from the Venetians during the reign of Mehmed IV. On the eastern front Baghdad was lost to the Safavids temporarily in 1623 and only with the military strength of Murad IV was it re-conquered in 1639. After this date a long peace with the Safavids was established.

Austria made allies with other European powers, including France, and began a struggle against the Ottomans. The Ottoman response resulted in the unsuccessful siege of Vienna in 1683 during the long reign of Mehmed IV and the loss of the Ottoman province of Hungary. The Carlowitz (Karlofça) treaty made after the battle in 1699 secured Hungary to the Austrians and the Morea to the Venetians. This was the most unfavorable treaty signed by the Ottomans up to that time.

Despite military losses, diplomatically the Ottoman Empire continued its relations with the European powers, which still considered the empire a powerful state with large resources.

The importance of Ottoman trade to the world economy declined due to the successes of the Atlantic trade, which brought huge supplies of silver, cotton, and sugar from the Americas. Thus the revenues of the Ottomans decreased and the value of the Ottoman silver coin fell sharply. The loss in the Ottoman monetary system resulted in an unsurpassed inflation, and unhappy military and state servants, whose salaries declined markedly in value. As a result they often resorted to revolts. The social system also suffered from the weakening economy as bribery and illegal stocking of goods tormented city life in Istanbul. The peasantry in Anatolia also rebelled for similar reasons.

The sultans were less directly concerned with the administration of the state and statesmen and generals became more prominent. Some of these men of *devşirme* origin (recruited) such as Sinan Pasha, Murad Pasha, Halil Pasha and three Köprülü family members became very influential in state politics. The royal women, especially the mothers of the sultans, such as the wife of Ahmed I and the mother of Murad IV, Kösem Sultan, and the mother of Mehmed IV, Turhan Sultan, were also more directly involved in politics since young sultans were often enthroned. The eunuchs of the palace were often part of the factions lead by powerful harem women. Sultans were enthroned and deposed untraditionally and many times by the pressure of the janissaries, who made alliances with various factions in the palace. The discipline in the recruitment and training of the janissaries was waning. Osman II, who tried to establish discipline among them, was deposed and killed by the janissaries. Murad IV in his late reign succeeded in raising a new military force alongside the janissaries.

Each Ottoman sultan was known for certain characteristics: Mehmed III (1595-1603) was the last of the Ottoman sultans who came to power after governing a province during his father's sultanate. He was also the first sultan after Süleyman I (the Magnificent) to go on military campaign. When he was enthroned, he killed nineteen princes who could have been contenders to the throne. This was the last time such a practice was employed and after him brothers of the enthroned sultan were kept alive but lived in confinement in the palace. The sons of the sultan were equally robbed of any public role and confined instead to the quarters of the palace. Mehmed's reign was marked by his mother Safiye Sultan's infringement upon state affairs.

Ahmed I (1603-1617) was merely 14 years old when he was enthroned and died at the early age of 28. Instead of his son, who was 13 years old, his brother Mustafa I (1617-18), who did not have a son and suffered from mental instability, became the sultan after him. This was the first example of the appointing of the brother of the sultan instead of his son. The reason for this shift is probably not only due to the young age of Ahmed's eldest son but also to the powerful factions in the palace behind Ahmed's concubine Kösem Sultan who had more then one candidate for the throne.

Osman II (1618-22) came to power at the age of 15 and had ambitions to bring discipline to the state affairs. His actions threatened many authorities and at the end caused his life to be taken at the hands of the janissaries. It was the first time an Ottoman sultan was deposed and killed by his 'servants', and the image of the untouchable sultan was lost forever.

Murad IV (1623-40) became the sultan at the age of 11 after the second reign of Mustafa I (1622-23). His mother Kösem Sultan was able to rule state affairs for a decade. Murad IV later resumed power in state affairs by establishing new laws and enforcing discipline and punishment. His reign also saw the abolishment of coffee and wine drinking as well as tobacco consumption. When he died in his late twenties he had no male heir thus his brother İbrahim I was enthroned.

İbrahim I (1640-48) was another Ottoman sultan who suffered from mental instability. His interest in Harem women benefited his mother Kösem Sultan who once again became powerful in state affairs. Her intrigues, financial squander, and harsh taxes marked İbrahim's reign. He was the second Ottoman sultan to have been deposed and killed.

Mehmed IV (1648-87) was six years old when he became the sultan. His mother Turhan Sultan arranged the killing of Kösem Sultan. The minting of the less valuable copper –silver coin and the revolts of the peasantry in Anatolia marked Mehmed's reign. He preferred to live in the Edirne Palace. A large fire in Istanbul consumed much of the city. The Köprülü family's involvement in state affairs as reliable grand viziers began during this time. Mehmed was deposed by rebellious troops and the powerful statesmen.

When Mehmed IV's brother Süleyman II (1687-91) was enthroned, he was 45 years old although he was just three-and-a-half months younger then Mehmed IV. He was not given even an honorary governorship of a province. 39 years of confinement was spent mostly in Edirne and Istanbul. When Süleyman II was enthroned, Mehmed IV was put in confinement in the same place where Süleyman was kept. During his reign the janissaries became unruly. Many gold and silver objects were melted to be given as money to pay for the janissaries. There was no safety in Istanbul due to constant rebellions and pillage. Janissaries even managed to get into the palace. Less valuable copper coins were issued. During Köprülü Fazıl Mustafa Pasha's grand vizierate, some military success and control over janissaries was achieved. Süleyman II did not have a son and died in Edirne.

Ahmed II (1691-95), who was Süleyman II's younger brother, was enthroned in Edirne at the age of 48 with the support of the grand vizier Fazıl Mustafa Pasha. Like his brother Süleyman, he spent 43 years in confinement in Istanbul. During his short reign, he never went to Istanbul. In Europe, battles with Venice, Austria, and Poland began. When the grand vizier died in campaign Ahmed II could not show much success in administration and died of illness four years later.

Mustafa II (1695-1703), who was also the son of Mehmed IV and brother of Süleyman II and Ahmed II, received a good education and joined his father in his hunting and campaigns in Europe. His confinement began when he was 23 years old. He was the last sultan who physically led the Ottoman army in a battle (in the Austrian campaign). He issued the first state coin with a *tuğra* in order to stop the circulation of low valued coins. He spent only eight months in Istanbul and resided in Edirne during the rest of his reign. His appointments created much disappointment and a large group that rebelled in Istanbul even went to Edirne. Under pressure Mustafa left the throne to his brother Ahmed III. When Mustafa IV was confined again he died after four months.

Architectural activity

Unlike the 16th century only two major monuments were built throughout the 17th century. The first one, the mosque complex of Ahmed I was built between 1609 and 1617 by the chief architect Mehmed Ağa (as chief architect 1606-22), who was trained by Sinan.

Until the mid-18th century no monumental mosque complex was built in Istanbul. The Sultan Ahmed Mosque complex included a hospital, a hospice, a public kitchen, public fountains, a Koran school, a market street, a bath, and the mausoleum of Ahmed I (not all buildings have survived). The second building, the Valide or New Mosque was begun by Safiye Sultan, the mother of Murad III, in 1597 but was not finished. The first architect was Davud, who was the chief architect after Sinan. When he died in 1598 Ahmed Ağa continued the building but it was stopped by Ahmed I at the ground level probably to allocate all the available resources to his own mosque complex. The building activity on the Valide Mosque was later resumed by another imperial woman, Turhan Sultan, the mother of Mehmed IV in the mid-17th century, and finished in 1663. The Valide Mosque complex included a royal pavilion, a primary school, a public fountain, a library, a market street, and Turhan's large mausoleum.

Both mosques were designed architecturally as larger variations on the classical Sinan mosques, namely the Şehzade Mosque. The Sultan Ahmed Mosque still has the largest interior space among all the mosques in Istanbul. The Sultan Ahmed and the Valide Mosque complexes are also the last large mosque complexes built in Ottoman architecture. However, the subsidiary buildings of the complexes are not connected to the mosque in an organic way. When both mosques were built, existing buildings posed a great difficulty in securing even the necessary empty lot for the mosques themselves. Thus, subsidiary buildings were arranged without an enclosure wall.

The Sultan Ahmed Mosque is decorated completely with tiles of various patterns (hence the modern word 'Blue Mosque'), but the decorative program shows that Iznik tile producers were no longer well coordinated with the central building activity.

The Valide Mosque was built in a restricted area very close to the water. The first architect Davud Ağa's ability to build a solid foundation close to the water allowed the mosque to withstand many earthquakes. The architect Mustafa Ağa completed the mosque in 1665.

Throughout the 17th century small buildings such as water dispensers and tombs were built. These buildings not only allowed their patrons to satisfy a public charity act without too much expense but also included the artistic trends of the century. During the reign of Murad IV, two large city markets (Vezir Hanı and Büyük Valide Hanı) were built in Istanbul. Mehmed IV built two palaces in Istanbul (Beşiktaş and Eyüp). These palaces are only known from historical records.

Decorative arts

The 17th century was more of a continuity of the 16th century in terms of Ottoman decorative arts. There were no new major styles. Instead, 16th century classical motifs continued to dominate the Ottoman decorative arts. Perhaps the lack of continuous patronage by the sultan and his close entourage in the arts was the cause of this subdued period. Some of the court workshops were closed or worked with fewer artists. Thus in this chapter only a few objects are chosen as examples to reflect a long time period. The only novelty in terms of style is seen on a small group of metal objects made for the court and influenced by European models in the second half of the 17th century.

Decorated manuscripts

Decorated manuscripts continued to be produced especially in the early 17th century during the reign of Mehmed III since many works were already in the production process by Lokman's team when Murad III died. An exceptional six volume manuscript about the life of the Prophet Muhammad

Fig. 58 Eğri Fetihnamesi, Topkapı Palace Museum, H. 1609, 68b-69a

(*Siyer-i Nebi* by Darir) illustrated with 814 miniatures was among them. Mehmed III replaced Lokman in 1597 as the court historiographer with Talikizade, who was already in Lokman's team and written works on contemporary Ottoman history in Turkish. Nakkaş Osman does not appear to continue to work after 1597. During the reign of Mehmed III, Talikizade wrote an epic history in Turkish on the military campaign of Mehmed III in Eger (Eğri), which he was also part of. Talikizade's work was illustrated soon after it was composed with four miniatures (1596-1600). In fact the miniatures, three of which are double-paged, were made untraditionally separately while the text was being copied. Thus the miniatures have a blank space behind them. One of the miniatures (Fig. 58 *Eğri Fetihnamesi*, Topkapı Palace Museum, H. 1609, 68b-69a) depicts the ceremonial entrance of Mehmed III into Istanbul from his victorious campaign in 1596. The Ottoman sultan Mehmed III and his vizier İbrahim Pasha are shown on horseback towards the middle of the scene. They are followed by other court officers who joined the sultan in his campaign as well as his household officers (*çuhadar* and *silahdar ağalar*) and a band of musicians (*mehteran*). In front of thc sultan we see the military units guarding the sultan and other statesmen. The procession is watched by the Safavid ambassador from Iran (shown standing on the top left) and his large entourage. Decorated textiles form a kind of blockade between the sultan's procession and the spectators. From the text we learn that the textiles were held by the textile merchants in the city (lower part of the miniature) and the entourage of the Safavid ambassador (shown on top). The pointed turbans of the Safavids clearly differ from the Ottoman ones. The manuscript was illustrated by Nakkaş Hasan, who was part of the royal household and received his training in the palace. At the end of the manuscript Talikizade and Nakkaş Hasan are shown at work. In this miniature, while Talikizade writes his text, a scribe copies it, and Nakkaş Hasan draws a composition with a very thin brush. The composition Hasan worked on belongs to the illustrated story of the life of the Prophet Muhammad mentioned above. Nakkaş Hasan also worked on the illumination of the famous Koran by Karahisari presented to Mehmed III after Murad III's death (see previous chapter). Nakkaş Hasan as evident from his later assumed title 'pasha' was appointed to various offices in the palace including the imperial vizierate. His services and artistic activity continued into the reign of Ahmed I as well. He is known to have made a large illuminated *tuğra* of Ahmed I.

During the reign of Ahmed I (1603-17), illustrated histories lost their appeal as there were less and less military victories to write about. (The last illustrated Ottoman history was produced later during the reign of Osman II (1618-22), who joined the army in its Hotin campaign). Instead albums (*murakka*), which included single paintings, became predominant. Kalender Pasha became the promoter of this type of manuscript. Kalender Pasha, who held various high-level court offices, is known to have been an illuminator, binder as well as a margin maker (*vassal*). An early example of such an album is attributed to circa 1610. In this album Kalender Pasha was asked to put together single paintings and calligraphic specimens of various sorts that were presented to the sultan. He describes in the preface of the album how he selected and put the paintings together by making illuminated margins. Portraits of the Ottoman sultans and examples from an illustrated history book are also placed in this album. On one of the pages (Fig. 59 Album page, Topkapı Palace Museum, B. 408, 8b) we see various single figures including the Ottoman sultan Murad III placed on the same page. The margins are decorated with wavy lines of the *çintemani* motif and *hatayis* in gold. Other pages from this album show depictions of dailylife and entertainment which clearly depart from the previous century's tastes.

Fig. 59 Album page, Topkapı Palace Museum, B. 408, 8b

Many other albums were produced during the course of the 17th century. Various European engravings in the baroque style, which entered the Ottoman palace at that time, were also placed in these albums. The Ottoman painters must have looked at and studied these images since there are some attempts to depict the third dimension in single paintings produced for albums as well.

As diplomatic and trade relations with Europe increased in the second half of the 17th century, European ambassadors and the painters who accompanied them illustrated Ottoman processions, Ottoman costumes, and daily life. Albums showing Ottoman costumes were also produced for them by the numerous Ottoman painters who were not on payroll but formed part of the relevant guilds of the city.

The illuminated manuscripts of the period continued 16th century motifs and page designs. Korans and prayer books display the best examples of this period. However, a decline in some of the colors' brightness as in dark blue is noticeable. Gilded surfaces also loose some of their glow. The motifs become larger and delicate draftsmanship is applied less.

Architectural decoration

In the 17th century Iznik tile (and ceramic) production faced a major decline. The tile producers encountered economic problems as they were forced to cater only to the needs of the Ottoman court. Under these pressures tile decoration lost its diversity and largely adhered to symmetric and repetitive motifs and designs, which were dominant in the 16th century. The cypress tree became a dominant motif. The flower motifs of the previous century such as tulips, carnations, jasmine, and roses continued to be applied on tiles. The famous red of the second half of the 16th century disappeared in the mid-17th century and turned into a brown tone. Glazes also lost their brilliance and strength after the mid-17th century. Duly the production in Iznik fell and disappeared completely by the end of the century. On the other hand, the other tile and ceramic center Kütahya continued its production by catering to the open market, including the Christian churches of the Ottoman Empire.

The Sultan Ahmed Mosque in Istanbul dated to the early 17th century provides a rich collection of the high quality tiles, which continued to be produced in the late 16th and early 17th century. Documents show that some of these tiles were made in Kütahya since Iznik itself was unable to produce the high number of tiles required for the mosque. Other good examples of the 17th century tile production from Iznik and Kütahya can be found in the Üsküdar Çinili Mosque built by Kösem Sultan in 1641, the sultan's kiosk in the Valide Mosque, and the Revan and Baghdad Kiosks of the Topkapı Palace (1636/1639) built by Murad IV after military victories in Baghdad and Erivan.

A tiled panel (Fig. 60 Tiled panel, Topkapı Palace Museum) dated to 1666 in the Valide Sultan ward of the Harem in the Topkapı Palace depicts an interesting view of the Kaaba. The panel consists of square tiles and features the Kaaba and the surrounding buildings in Mecca. It also includes the names of the buildings. The buildings are shown from various perspectives, common in manuscript illustrations. The tiled panel exceptionally gives the name of the artist Ali Iskenderiye *teberdar-ı hassa*, who belonged to the rank of halberdiers (*baltacılar*) at the court, and the Muslim year 1077 (=1666) when it was made. In 1665 a large fire burnt the harem in the Topkapı Palace. Some of the present decoration must have belonged to the decoration made after that fire. Blue and turquoise dominates the panel with minor inclusions of red and black. It is not known whether the specific tile panel was made in Iznik or Kütahya. Ali Iskenderiye was

Fig. 60 Tiled panel, Topkapı Palace Museum

most likely an artist at the court and could have drawn a cartoon for the panel, which was then applied on tiles. It appears that the same cartoon was used to make the tiles for the *mihrab* of the black eunuchs' mosque in the Topkapı Palace. Two tile panels, which came from specific mosques in Edirne and Bursa now in the Istanbul Turkish and Islamic Arts Museum (Inv. 827 and 830), attest that similar tile panels were also placed in the interior of the public mosques in later times. The design of the panel seems to be related to the depictions made specifically for the certificates of the hajj pilgrims, which were made even before the Ottomans.

Textiles

Although the number of textile makers in the court workshops decreased as in many other branches of art, textile production did not show a drastic decline like the Iznik tiles and ceramics. Only a type of the brocaded silks (*kemha*), which were almost a monopoly of the court workshops, showed a sudden decline. But the velvets of Bursa or other valuable textiles produced in the city by the guilds continued to be made in the 17th century. They were exported as well. The motifs of the 16th century also continued but larger patterns and more standardization were applied. Rosettes, fan shapes, and the crescent became more predominant on the velvets. The use of gold and silver as part of the textiles was also attested less and perhaps due to the lack of sufficient gold and silver reserves, yellow and ivory colored threads were used in their place. Towards the end of the century we also see more of small repeat motifs and notice a technical decline. Russian collections, which are rich in Ottoman textiles, also provide clues for the dating of certain textiles and motifs.

Metalwork

The mid-17th century saw the appearance of a new flower style in Ottoman decorative arts. Exceptionally, unlike previous Ottoman styles, its forerunners first appeared in metalwork instead of arts of the book. Silver objects such as clocks, boxes, and incense burners made for the palace were decorated with this new flower style. The most distinctive character of the new flowers is that their center is crisscrossed and the petals have a voluminous effect. Examples of the style first appear on European clocks of the 17th century. It is likely that this European-influenced style was brought to the Ottoman decorative repertoire by European clock makers. This new flower style was applied on various metal objects in the Ottoman palace until the mid-18th century when more

Fig. 61 Topkapı Palace Museum, 53/86

European motifs entered the Ottoman repertoire. An example of it can be shown on the gilded silver wall clock made by an artist named Bulugat, perhaps of Central European origin (Fig. 61 Topkapı Palace Museum, 53/86). He signed his name in the back of the clock. The clock's dial, which is 18cm in diameter, is made entirely in the openwork technique and decorated with the new flower style. It is completely gilded. The clock is one of the earliest clocks in the Topkapı Palace. This and a few other clocks in the Topkapı collection have only the hour hand. A record dated to 1649 in the Topkapı Palace archive shows that clock makers Mehmed Abdullah Saati and Alemşah Saati are cited among the 24 jewelers and goldsmiths of the palace. Written sources indicate that Murad III received an Austrian clock with automatic moving figures. The earliest Ottoman-made clock was produced during his reign to indicate the hours of the prayer. No Ottoman clock has survived from the 16th century. European clocks were sent as diplomatic gifts or purchased by the Ottomans directly. 17th century European clock makers established themselves in the Galata district of Istanbul, where European and local artists are known to have worked together.

Chapter 7

A new cultural orientation and Influences of Europe on Ottoman art: 1703-1807

Historical setting

In the 18th century six Ottoman sultans reigned: Ahmed III (1703-1730), Mahmud I (1730-54), Osman III (1754-57), Mustafa III (1757-74), Abdülhamid I (1774-89), and Selim III (1789-1807). Except for Osman III, who only ruled for three years, the sultans reigned relatively long years. The first and the last sultans of the century, Ahmed III and Selim III, were deposed by the janissaries.

After the unfavorable peace treaty of Carlowitz in 1699, the Ottoman Empire continued to loose land slowly but there were no major losses until the 1770's. The beginning of the century was marked by the emergence of a new power, Russia. Ahmed III (1703-1730), who was the brother of Mustafa, was enthroned in Edirne at the age of 29 after 16 years of confinement in the Edirne and Istanbul palaces. During his early reign, the Ottomans succeeded in defeating the Russians and a treaty was signed in 1713. The Ottomans then began a campaign in Morea and regained it from the Venetians. The third assault of the Ottomans against Austria, however, resulted in losses in Hungary, Serbia, Belgrade, and the unfavorable treaty of Pasarowitzs, which was signed in 1718. The treaty, however, marked the beginning of a period of peace in the west, which lasted until 1730. During these years under the guidance of the grand vizier İbrahim Pasha (in office 1718-

30) diplomatic relations became important and the Ottomans sent for the first time ambassadors to Vienna in 1729, Paris in 1720-21, Moscow in 1722-23, and Warsaw in 1730. The purpose of these trips was to learn about new developments in Europe in science, military science, culture, and institutions. Sultan Ahmed III's own interests in gardens and outdoor entertainment found a convenient resonance in French city life (of the era of Louis XV) explained by the Ottoman ambassador Çelebi Mehmed. The Sultan and his vizier (and son-in-law) İbrahim Pasha erected new palaces on the scenic shores of the Golden Horn and the Bosphorus. Gardens were designed with cascading waterfalls and a period of leisurely life, celebrations and outdoor parties dominated court life. The Ottoman elite, namely the court officials, merchants of international trade, and landowners imitated the life style of the sultan and his vizier as well. There was an increase in artistic and literary activities as part of this leisurely life. This period 1718-30 is also known as Tulip Period due to the interest in cultivating various types of tulips to be planted in the gardens. The first Ottoman print was established in 1727 (the European one was established in 1440) after ones seen in Paris. Military consultants were invited from France for the building of powerful cannons.

In 1730 the eastern frontiers of the empire were threatened by the Safavid Shah Tahmasp II. The Ottoman vizier İbrahim Pasha wanted to wage war but the janissaries revolted and a series of rebellions followed in Istanbul, which resulted in the execution of the vizier and the deposition of the sultan. These rebellions are also interpreted as the resistance of a group of traditionalists against changes in social life promoted by Ahmed III and his vizier. Despite the enthronement of the new sultan Mahmud I (1730-54), the janissaries continued their rebellions and destroyed the newly constructed palaces and gardens in Istanbul. In the end Mahmud I secretly had their leader Patrona Halil killed.

Mahmud I followed the Ottoman army's campaigns in Georgia and Iran from his palace in Istanbul. Although the Ottomans succeeded in acquiring important cities in Georgia and Iran, soon new problems arose and a treaty signed in 1736 forced the Ottomans to return these new domains back to the Safavids ruled by Nadir Shah. The Russians in the same year made advances in Crimea and took the important castle of Azak.

With a new alliance with Russia the Austrians attacked the Ottomans on their western front in 1737. The Ottomans responded with an attack on Belgrade. In the end a favorable treaty was signed in Belgrade in 1739 and the Austrians gave back what they had gained in the Pasarowitz Treaty. A period of peace ensued with the Russians until 1768 and with the Austrians until 1788.

Although new attacks lead by the Safavid Shah Nadir started, the Ottoman response stopped them from any gains and a further treaty made in 1746 repeated one that was signed in 1639.

The relatively long peaceful period from 1746 to 1768 during the reigns of Mahmud I 1730-54, Osman III (1754-57) and Mustafa III (1757-74) coincided with internal conflicts amongst the European powers. Mahmud I came to power at the age of thirty-six after twenty-seven years of confinement in the Topkapı Palace. He was succeeded by Osman III, who came to power at the age of 55 after 51 years of confinement in the Topkapı Palace. His reign only lasted three years until his death. Both Mahmud I and Osman III did not have any heirs thus their brother Mustafa III came to power at the age of 40 after 27 years of confinement. He and his grand vizier Ragıp Pasha started a series of reforms in the military to prepare for the impending dangers of Russia. With a false sense of readiness, however, the Ottomans confronted the Russians and lost on many fronts. With their victory, the Russians ruled by

Katherine the Great managed to control the areas that opened the way for their navy to navigate to the Mediterranean and destroyed the Ottoman navy. Perhaps more importantly, in 1771 they attacked Crimea on the Black Sea coast. When Mustafa III died, Abdülhamid I became the sultan at the age of 49 after spending 44 years in confinement in the palace. During his reign the Ottoman army continued unsuccessfully defending its Black Sea domains against the Russian army. The following treaty (Küçük Kaynarca) signed in 1774 became the worst one signed by the Ottomans up to that date. Accordingly, Crimea became an independent state. The Russians were allowed to keep an ambassador at all times in Istanbul and have an orthodox church as a protectorate of the Orthodox population in Istanbul. Eventually, the Russians extended these rights to all the orthodox populations of the empire.

Selim III became the 28th sultan at the age of 18 after 15 years of confinement but since he was the first born Ottoman prince in the last 36 years he was allowed to spend his confinement years in relative freedom during the reign of his uncle Abdülhamid. Selim immersed himself in music and poetry during this time. His reign was marked by a renewed interest in reforming the military, administration, social, and economic life. Permanent embassies were established in Paris, London, Vienna, and Berlin. Foreign educators were brought to teach in the newly established imperial engineering school. Rebellions for independence by the Ottoman governors in the Ottoman provinces, especially in the Arab ones, became a growing concern. In 1789 Napoleon invaded Egypt. This had dire consequences for the Ottoman Empire, not only politically but also economically. Although the events were reversed in 1801, Selim and his reforms, especially the new military ranks were not received with acceptance by the traditionalists. Feeling the pressure from the janissaries, Selim resigned but could not escape from an execution by court servants at the request of the janissaries a year later.

From the Ottoman point of view, the 18th century can be regarded as a period of change and resistance, which was unable to match the unprecedented developments in Europe, especially in technology and industry.

Architectural activity

The 18th century, particularly during the reign of Ahmed III, is remembered mostly for its civil architecture. Ahmed III was fond of outdoor living and garden entertainment perhaps more than any other Ottoman sultan. He often gathered poets and artists at his court. He cultivated existing palace gardens and repaired or built pavilions and small palaces along the Golden Horn and the Bosphorus. Plans of gardens and palaces were brought from Paris for this purpose. With these in mind, the court architect Mehmed Ağa turned the Kağıthane brook in the Golden Horn into a cascading canal with marble quays. The sultan's pavilion called the Sadabad was built by vizier İbrahim Pasha at the end of the canal where a large pool was made. In the 1720's 170 pavilions were built just along the Kağıthane district according to historical records. Unfortunately none has survived due to the destruction of the pavilions after the demise of İbrahim pasha. Examples of other building activity along the Bosphorus have not survived either due to light and perishable materials or further rebuilding in consequent years. For example the present day 19th century Dolmabahçe Palace was erected in the location of the former Beşiktaş Palace built by Selim III (1789-1807) in the 18th century.

Ahmed III, who was also a poet and calligrapher, built a separate library building in the Topkapı Palace in 1719, which still survives. He also built two independent fountains in front of the Topkapı Palace (see below) and Üsküdar in 1728. The new use of the fountain as an architectural entity and as a focal point of public space marked the beginning of a long series of similar fountains built in the 18th century. From 1729 to 1746 a total of 32 fountain buildings, and from 1751 to 1807, 31 were erected by various patrons including those outside the court.

Among the public buildings erected in the 18th century the Nuruosmaniye Mosque complex begun by Mahmud I in 1739 and completed by Osman III in 1756 constitutes the first large religious complex of the century. It stands directly across from the covered bazaar and includes a library, tomb, public kitchen, and public fountains. Architecturally it is an example of the baroque and rococo influenced Ottoman architecture that became predominant towards the mid-18th century in Istanbul. Its architect is thought to be Simeon Kalfa who was a Greek architect at the service of the Ottoman court. Its horseshoe-shaped courtyard (still the only example in Turkey), prominent arches and profiles on the exterior supporting the large dome, and circular *mihrab* extending from the building proper are the new applications that clearly depart from classical Ottoman architecture and betray ideas taken from the baroque style in Europe. Its large windows were designed with the imported products of the new glass industry established in Europe. The building signals a new beginning in Ottoman architecture and also the beginning of the dominance of Christian architects in Ottoman architecture. The Laleli Mosque built between 1760-1764 by Mustafa III and the Beylerbeyi Mosque built in 1778 by Abdülhamid I are other examples of baroque and rococo influenced Ottoman architecture. Other mosques and smaller buildings like libraries, schools, and tombs built by the imperial family and statesmen followed these new developments in architecture. While traditional plans and building types were used, the individual forms of the architectural elements and the overall decoration had direct influences from the European baroque and rococo styles. Thus this type of Ottoman architecture is conveniently called Turkish baroque or Turkish rococo. The end of the century was marked by large military buildings built in the neo-classical style during the reign of Selim III. Selimiye, Ayazaağa, Tophane, and Kuleli barracks are examples of European building types that were to serve the new Ottoman military.

Decorative arts

The 18th century can be seen as the beginning of a new era in Ottoman art, in which Ottoman taste was no longer guided by the Islamic (Timurid or Ottoman) mode but by a distinctly European one. The change in decorative arts was felt first in the mid-17th century in the decoration of Ottoman clocks- an object of European invention- as we have seen in the previous chapter. With the increased flow of European goods into the Ottoman palace in the 18th century a taste for a European lifestyle slowly took effect in the palace and upper classes of the Ottoman society. The love of leisurely life reflected in the garden parties of the Ahmed III era was translated into an abundant vocabulary of flowers and fruits in Ottoman decorative arts. Flowers and fruits drawn in a naturalistic manner spread to every imaginable surface in Ottoman decorative arts from manuscript pages to prayer rugs. Once the inhibition towards European lifestyle and technology were lifted among the predominantly Muslim taste makers of the Empire (namely the sultan, imperial family, statesmen, wealthy merchants and land owners), the influence of European art never stopped and continued with an increased rate in the 19th and 20th centuries. Thus the 18th century can be seen as a time period when European baroque and rococo styles were fused with traditional Ottoman forms and functions.

Architectural decoration

A room in the Topkapı Palace, known as the fruit room of Ahmed III, (Fig. 62 Topkapı Palace Museum, Fruit room of Ahmed III) is an early example of a style that came to dominate the early 18th century. The small square room built by Ahmed III in 1705 most likely as a dining room is completely painted with flower and fruit motifs in lacquer on wood. Various flower arrangements in vases and heaps of fruits in large bowls decorate the wooden surfaces of the entire room. Rows of small calligraphic panels of poetry also compliment the decoration. The ceiling is decorated with a large mirror and the edges of the ceiling are decorated with cypresses and oval medallions filled with stylized flowers in the traditional sense, but the flower depictions between the cypresses and the medallions reflect the new flower style. Although the use of flowers and fruits had been a typical decoration for Islamic palaces for a long time, here the style brings three dimension and naturalism to the same motifs. Similar types of fruit and flower decoration can be found in many objects throughout the 18th century but its early use in this room shows that Ahmed III and the painters (*nakkaş*) of the court were still influential in its dissemination.

Fig. 62 Topkapı Palace Museum, Fruit room of Ahmed III

A slightly later use of the same decorative repertoire can be found on the fountain of Ahmed III in front of the Topkapı Palace (Fig. 63 The fountain of Ahmed III). The fountain built in 1728 by Ahmed III includes highly decorated facades on

Fig. 63 The fountain of Ahmed III

all sides. The wide eaves of the roof bring a touch of pavilion architecture to the fountain. The facades are decorated with niches and arches derived from traditional forms, but the curved corners of the fountain and the high relief acanthus leaves decorating the friezes are new additions to Ottoman architecture. The decoration of the fountain with calligraphic panels and floral designs are not new but the motifs used in the floral decoration, namely the large floral bouquets in vases carved in stone, are new applications on the facades of Ottoman buildings. The use of tiles is kept to a minimum. Unlike the stone decoration of the fountain, the tiles still use 16th century motifs. A band of repeat tiles decorated with *çintemani* motifs and cloud bands on a white ground surrounds the fountain on all sides in the upper part of the fountain. These tiles were made in the Tekfursarayı workshops in Istanbul, where a revived tile production can be documented to have taken place at least in the first part of the 18th century. The tiles of the workshops, which were set up by İbrahim Pasha, vizier of Ahmed III, in the early part of the 18th century, however, could not match the quality of the Iznik tiles as they were thick and clotted. After a few applications in Istanbul, the workshops closed after İbrahim Pasha's death due to economic hardship and lack of patronage.

In fact, tile decoration slowly disappeared from the decoration of Ottoman buildings to be replaced by brushwork decoration. Thus Kütahya workshops, which continued to produce tiles (as well as ceramics) in the 17th and 18th centuries, produced smaller scale projects mostly in the provinces.

The smaller fountain of Ahmed III at Üsküdar also displays a similar type of stonework decoration to that of the Topkapı fountain but excludes the tiles. The fountain built by Mahmud I in 1732 in Tophane district was even more embellished than the fountains built by Ahmed III. Its carved stone decoration includes a high relief frieze of fruit trees set in vases separated by columns under the roof and also in and around main niches on the facades. The stylized floral decoration in relief includes acanthus leaves and displays a marked distance from classical Ottoman motifs. The decoration was also painted in various colors and gilded although none has survived today.

In several fountains built throughout the 18th century after the 1740's rococo forms took over the traditional Ottoman repertoire in design and decoration. Influenced by the French rococo style dominant during the reign of Louis XV in France, the Turkish rococo decoration included curved surfaces, various curved arch shapes, cartouches, cornices, plasters, acanthus leaves, and shell shapes. The fountain of Abdülhamid I in Sirkeci dated to 1777 and the fountain of Mihrişah Valide Sultan (mother of Selim III) built in Eyüp in 1795 are large-scale examples of rococo architecture. Designed and decorated with these new shapes these public Ottoman fountains built in various districts of Istanbul provided a new dynamic appearance amongst traditional city buildings.

The almost drastic change in the Ottoman decorative repertoire towards the French rococo must have been led by the Ottoman court. It is known that drawings were brought from France and that new examples of rococo influenced Ottoman decoration were first applied in the Topkapı Palace itself. Several rooms in the palace were redesigned in this fashion starting from the mid-18th century: Pavilion of Osman III, hall of the throne (*hünkar sofası*), apartments (*hasoda*) of Abdülhamid I and Selim III, and several fountains and fireplaces of the palace. European baroque and rococo styles are evident in curvy cartouches, s- and c- shaped arches, acanthus or shell motifs, blossoming branches surrounding columns with Ionic or Corinthian capitals, flower bouquets, landscapes seen through tasseled curtains, and still-life paintings of flowers and fruits. This new repertoire was applied in brushwork decoration on wood and plaster. Until the 18th century brushwork decoration shared a common decorative vocabulary with the other arts of the period such as decorated manuscripts, tiles, metalwork, woodwork, and textiles. Towards the mid-18th century however the idea of wall painting penetrated into brushwork decoration and in addition to the shared vocabulary with other decorative arts of the period, landscapes became a common form of decoration. Landscapes drawn from a perspectival view with a source of light and still-lives with tonal rendering to indicate the third dimension reflect the idea of wall paintings in the European sense. The human figure was still absent in all paintings during this time. Figures were commonly applied in high levels of the walls under the ceilings and domes. The Bosphorus and Golden Horn landscapes of Istanbul with pavilions near rivers became a common feature of the repertoire (Fig. 64 Wall painting, Topkapı Palace Harem). In this slightly later work from the Topkapı Palace we see a large pavilion with cascading pools built near a river. In the distance there are other large-scale buildings built on the water. On the far left where the river must meet the sea we see steamboats. Somewhat imaginary but alluding to Kağıthane region of the Golden Horn, the painting reflects this favorite theme of the period. The steamboat, which

Fig. 64 Wall painting, Topkapı Palace Harem

was introduced to Istanbul in the early 19th century, dates the painting to that period. Interestingly this landscape repertoire, which was first used in the palace, also found a receptive environment in the decorations of the mansions and even mosques built outside of Istanbul. These paintings included views of Istanbul (sometimes imaginary), which showed the pavilions built in Kağıthane and the shores of the Bosphorus. Obviously the desires of the local elites in the leisurely life of Istanbul (similar to that of the famed Tulip Era) were reflected in these paintings.

Decorated manuscripts and works on paper

Decorated manuscripts of the 18th century differed from the previous centuries not only in the style of the decorations on bindings and illuminations but also in the subjects of manuscripts. A known artist of the 18th century was Ali Üsküdari (d. 1763). Ali Üsküdari was an artist of lacquer painting, manuscript painting, and illumination who worked on a variety of objects. His signature is preserved on some of his works. His lacquer work decorated bindings, pen boxes, writing boards, writing chests, and bows on materials such as leather, wood and cardboard. In his works we see that while he kept many of the classical 16th century motifs like the serrated leaves of the *saz* style, he gives a voluminous appearance to the same traditional motifs and also includes the new Europeanized flower style of this period. A lacquered writing board he made for Mustafa III (1757-74) is a good example of his mature style (Fig.65 Lacquered writing board, Topkapı Palace Museum, CY 413). In the main field of this board we see a bouquet of flowers with minute details and shading as an example of the new flower style. At the same time we see the traditional '*saz*' motifs around this bouquet and also in the wide borders surrounding the main field. The other side of the board is also decorated and includes the dedication to Mustafa III, Hijri date 1171 (=1757), and the name of the artist as a signature. The new flower style on the binding can also be seen in a much earlier work of Üsküdari dated to 1727. This poetry album in Turkish consists of numerous paintings of flowers made in the same style. Thus we can say that the new flower style began to be seen in manuscripts in the earlier part of the 18th century.

The themes of the illustrated manuscripts of the 18th century continued the new path opened in the 17th century. There were no glorious military feats to illustrate, however, the new interest in the daily pleasures of life was well reflected in the decorated manuscripts of the period. Abdülcelil Çelebi of Edirne, also known as Levni, (means colorful in Arabic), was the best known *nakkaş* of the first half of the 18th century. He was a contemporary and companion of Ahmed

Fig.65 Lacquered writing board, Topkapı Palace Museum, CY 413

III. Levni had already worked for the previous sultan Mustafa II in Edirne before he came to Istanbul. A series of portraits of the Ottoman sultans, which he began in Edirne, was completed with the inclusion of Ahmed III and presented to him. In these portraits Levni employs a setting that makes the portraits of the sultans look more alive. For example, Ahmed III is shown seated on a decorated throne with his son standing next to him. The sultan and the prince wear similar costumes. The detailed facial features of the portraits give them a natural appearance.

A painting from another work of Levni best illustrates the leisurely atmosphere of the Ahmed III era. This painting, which is from an album that consists of 48 portraits of single figures from the Ottoman court, is signed by Levni. (Fig. 66 Album page, Topkapı Palace Museum, H. 2164, 17b) In this painting Levni depicts four female musicians seated under an arch. Their costumes and headresses clearly show the fashion of the time at the court. In fact the open collars of the women worn by the *tambur* (lute) player in the miniature have been mentioned in history books as something common during this period. Some of the later sultans did not approve of this fashion and tried to stop Muslim women from wearing such clothes.

Fig. 66 Album page, Topkapı Palace Museum, H. 2164, 17b

Levni's most celebrated work is the *Surname* (festival book) of Vehbi dated to 1727. The manuscript describes the

1720 circumcision festival of Ahmed III's four sons (Fig. 67 *Surname-i Vehbi*, Topkapı Palace Museum, A 3593, 92b-93a). The festival which lasted 15 days and nights in the Okmeydanı district of Istanbul and the waterside pavilions is described in detail in the text by the author Vehbi, who was part of the festivities. Levni and his assistants illustrated the text with 137 double-page miniatures in detail. Compared to the 17th century, obviously this was a revival in the illustrated history genre but here, instead of the ostentatious display of the Ottoman Empire's power and richness evident in the 16th century *Surname* of the Murad III period, the enjoyable side of the festival was emphasized. Thus not only the processions of the guilds but the festivities in the Golden Horn are lavishly depicted. Levni employs color shading and a somewhat perspectival viewpoint in his miniatures and uses the double page as a continuous surface to depict large events with numerous figures in them. The double-page miniature on 92b-93a depicts the ropedancers above the water. The sultan, his two sons, and the accompanying court servants watch the festivities from their Aynalıkavak Pavilion (built right on the edge of the water) in the top left

Fig. 67 Surname-i Vehbi, Topkapı Palace Museum, A 3593, 92b-93a

corner of the miniature. The vizier İbrahim Pasha and other statesmen watch the event from a large boat on the right. Three foreign ambassadors are shown in a smaller boat below them. Other guests, musicians, and dancers are shown in other boats. As explained in the text, first a chariot with a model woman in it is pulled on the double ropes attached to a large tree on the shore and the masts of the boats. After this, male dancers perform on small platforms hidden beneath their long skirts and securely attached to the dancers through a mechanism. In the text it is explained that when the dancers completed their performances in front of the sultan, they dropped to the sea and started swimming. The perspectival depiction of the large boat on the bottom left, the walls around the pavilion, and the tonal rendering of the trees show Levni's new approach to painting. In a way his style reminds us of some of the comparable attempts seen in the miniatures from the reign of Bayezid II, perhaps resulting from similar close contacts with Europe.

After the *Surname* Ottoman sultans no longer commissioned manuscripts for their private treasury or sponsored historical manuscripts. Instead topics related to the social life of the period were chosen to be illustrated. Single-page miniatures collected in albums also continued to be favored. Another known artist of the 18th century Abdullah Buhari (active between 1726 and 1745) produced single-figure paintings and flower depictions. In a single-figure painting in an album (Fig. 68 Album page, Topkapı Palace Museum, YY 1043) Buhari depicts a daring subject for his time, a nude female in a Turkish

Fig. 68 Album page, Topkapı Palace Museum, YY 1043

bath. The woman is shown pouring water over herself next to the Turkish-style marble basin. The details of her body, hair, and jewels as well as the details of her waistcloth show the fine drawing skills of Buhari. The perspective lines of the marble floor revetments and the foreshortened basin indicate the artist's nontraditional painting style. Buhari also made single-flower paintings and landscapes.

Metalwork

A spectacular object from the Topkapı collection (Fig. 69 Dagger, Topkapı Palace Museum, 2/160) dated to 1746-7 is another example of the application of the new decorative vocabulary. The dagger and its sheath were originally made as a gift by the Ottoman Sultan Mahmud I (1730-54) for the Safavid Shah Nadir of Iran. While the gifts were en route Nadir Shah was assassinated and the embassy returned to the Ottoman palace with the gifts. The dagger, which has a small hidden English watch on its pommel, is decorated with large emeralds. The golden sheath is decorated with rose-cut and table-

Fig. 69 Dagger, Topkapı Palace Museum, 2/160

cut diamonds. The surface of the sheath is decorated with voluminous scrolls, and a colorful depiction of a basket of fruit is painted in enamel inside a cartouche. Mahmud I intended to send

Fig. 70 Prayer rug, Topkapı Palace Museum, 31/514

this dagger as a gift in response to the large throne he received from Nadir Shah. Similar jeweled objects in Russian collections indicate that the Ottomans used similar items as diplomatic gifts for other countries as well.

Textiles

Textile production, which was in decline in the 18th century relative to the previous centuries, continued with the applications of the new motifs on existing textile types. Silver brocaded textiles were banned by Ahmed III in the early 18th century although court consumption was left out of this ban as before. The miniatures of Levni (see fig. 66) depict mostly plain robes or robes with small patterns. Towards the middle of the 18th century the new European style became more visible in textiles and embroideries. A prayer rug from the end of the 18th century (Fig. 70 Prayer rug, Topkapı Palace Museum, 31/514) is decorated with a niche motif which was commonly used in the prayer carpets of the 16th and 17th centuries. Here the niche itself is shown as an arch placed on four columns. A lamp is shown hanging from the niche. Below the niche flowering plants sprout from a vase. The elements of the arch are made of intertwined branches of flowers shown in various shades. The wide border is decorated with dense scrollwork and large voluminous flowers. The rug is made of a red woolen cloth called Lahuraki (probably to indicate a similarity with the Indian works from Lahor) and embroidered with silver and colored silk threads. This and similar types of embroidered cloths were woven in the Tepebaşı looms of Istanbul. The decorative repertoire clearly indicates the wide acceptance of European styles and motifs even on religious items like the prayer rugs. What existed as stylized forms like the niche or the columns in the Ottoman decorative repertoire in the earlier centuries are here transformed into a Europeanized repertoire suggesting 'an observed environment'.

بسم الله الرحمن الرحيم
أبو بكر
عمر
عثمان
علي
وما أرسلناك إلا رحمة للعالمين
لولاك لولاك لما خلقت الأفلاك

Chapter 8

Departure from the past: 1807-1922

Historical setting

The 19th and early 20th centuries can be regarded politically as a period of constant loss of Ottoman territories and at the same time a period of reforms that eventually lead to the fall of the Ottoman dynasty and the establishment of a national Turkish state in 1922. During this last century of the Ottomans eight sultans reigned: Mustafa IV (1807-1808), Mahmud II (1808-39), Abdülmecid (1839-61), Abdülaziz I (1861-76), Murad V (1876), Abdülhamid II (1876-1909), Mehmed V Reşad (1909-18), and Mehmed VI Vahdeddin (1918-22). The reigns of Mustafa IV, Murad V, and Vahdeddin were quite short.

The earlier part of the 19th century was marked by the establishment of various reforms by Mahmud II. The military reforms, which had been first unsuccessfully attempted by Selim III, were enforced by Mahmud II on the janissaries by force and ended with numerous killings of the janissaries in 1826 (even their tombstones in the city could not escape) and the singling out of the Bektashi dervish order to which the janissaries adhered. Mahmud II's other reforms are considered to be the modernization of the Otoman administration and society. The reforms included the establishment of the press (the previous one was destroyed in 1807) and the printing of the first Ottoman newspaper in 1824, the creation of the first medical school in 1827, and the first military academy and imperial orchestra in 1833. Mahmud II also introduced European-style clothing and uniforms.

Mahmud II's centralist administration over the semi-independent local governors of the Ottoman Empire resulted in nationalist reactions in the provinces. Greece declared its independence in 1830 and others followed.

Abdülmecid became the sultan at the young age of 17. His early reign was marked by another important event: the declaration of *Tanzimat (1839)*, a human rights bill within the Ottoman Empire. According to this new political and social system, all the citizens within the Ottoman Empire gained equal political and civil rights under the authority of the Ottoman government. A similar declaration protecting the rights of the non-Muslims in 1856 further limited the power of the Ottoman government and the sultan over the non-Muslims of the empire and allowed European countries to interfere with Ottoman politics.

Europeanization of the Ottoman administration continued in the period after *Tanzimat* during the reigns of Abdülmecid (1839-61) and Abdülaziz (1861-76). During the Crimean war, which began in 1853 with Russian attacks, the Ottomans allied with the British and the French. Thousands of British and French soldiers came to Istanbul before and after the battle with the Russians in Crimea. At the end of the war the territorial rights of the Ottoman state were accepted.

The second half of the 19th century was less successful and the loss of territories continued as the former Ottoman provinces declared independence one by one. In 1875 the Ottomans declared bankruptcy as they were unable to pay their debts to European banks. A year later the first Ottoman constitution was declared.

Abdülhamid II's reign (1876-1909) was a period of further problems within the empire. The Ottomans lost control of the Balkans. Tunisia passed to the French, and Cypress and Egypt to the British. In 1881 a council of administration of the Ottoman public debt was formed. Seeing it as a threat to his existence Abdülhamid II abolished the *Tanzimat* rules and ruled with despotism, but the intellectual middle class that grew out of the *Tanzimat* era enforced the restoration of the constitution in 1908. The reign of Mehmed V (1909-18) was marked with unsuccessful wars against the Italians in North Africa, and against Bulgarians, Serbians, and Greeks in the Balkans. And finally in World War I, which began in 1914, the Ottomans allied with the Germans, and despite their success in Gallipoli, the Ottomans lost the war. During the reign of Mehmed VI (1918-22) the Arab territories of the empire passed to the British forces in 1919. The Ottomans were also forced to retreat from the Caucasus. When Istanbul was occupied by allied European powers in 1918 the representatives of the Ottoman sultan were compelled to sign the treaty of Sevres in which the remaining Ottoman territory including Istanbul passed to the control of the European powers. The growing success of the nationalist movement lead by Mustafa Kemal Atatürk, however, abolished the Ottoman government that signed the treaty and after its own War of Independence against the allied powers the present day Republic of Turkey was established in 1923. Sultan Vahdeddin left the country. Abdülmecid Efendi could not become a sultan but was allowed to remain as the caliph until 1924. After that date all existing members of the Ottoman dynasty were expelled out of Turkey and the political existence of the dynasty came to an end.

Architectural activity

The Ottoman sultans continued to build mosques and tombs throughout the 19th century. The Nusretiye (victory) Mosque in Tophane district was built by Mahmud II in 1826. The name refers to the victory of the sultan over the rebellious janissaries and the location of the mosque marks the end of the parade ground of the new artillery barracks. It was built by the imperial architect Kirkor Balian, the first of the family of Armenian architects that dominated the imperial Ottoman architecture of the 19th century. The Nusretiye and the Ortaköy mosques built by Abdülmecid in 1854 are examples of the baroque influenced Ottoman architecture. Teşvikiye Mosque also built by Abdülmecid in 1855 has more of a neoclassical appearance. Hamidiye Mosque built by Abdülhamid II inside the Yıldız Palace has influences even from church architecture in its planning and shows the liberty of choices of its architect, Sarkis Balian with approval from Abdülhamid II.

Among the tombs of the century the baroque influenced Nakşidil Sultan Tomb (mother of Mahmud II) dated to 1818, and neoclassical (French Empire style) styled Mahmud II's Tomb built in 1840 can be mentioned.

Ottoman sultans also built several new palaces to serve their new European way of living and entertainment. The Balian family of architects was influential in their design and heavy decoration, which departed drastically from traditional Ottoman forms as they were eclectically copied from European styles. Dolmabahçe Palace, which was built by the architect Garabed Balian in 1853 during the reign of Abdülmecid, was designed on a neoclassical plan but with heavy baroque decoration not witnessed in any European building itself. Foreign craftsmen and furnishings were used in its decoration. As a building it was the opposite of the Topkapı Palace in its planning and decoration. Çırağan Palace (now serving as a hotel after a fire and a large rebuilding) was built by Nigoğos Balian in 1863, and the Beylerbeyi Palace was built by Sarkis Balian in 1865. Both buildings were built for Abdülaziz in neoclassical style, which was less ornate than the decoration of the Dolmabahçe. The last building in the Topkapı Palace, Mecidiye Kiosk (now used as part of the restaurant in the museum today) was also built by Sarkis Balian. All of these buildings display the eclectic use of styles directly imported from Europe, which dominated the architecture of the period.

More military barracks and related buildings were built (or rebuilt in stone) in the 19th century, following those built by Selim III. The original wooden Selimiye barracks erected by Selim III in Haydarpaşa were rebuilt in stone in 1828 by Mahmud II. Three more sides were added by Abdülmecid in 1842 and 1853. This enormous building including a mosque, residential units for high rank military personnel, bath, shops, school, library, and a press, dominates the skyline on the Asia side above the Marmara Sea. The building also served the English army as a halting point and hospital during the Crimean war in the 19th century.

The changes in Ottoman life mainly in administration, education, and finance required new types of buildings to be built as well. This large building activity was also regulated by new rules. The newly established directorate of imperial buildings assumed the roles of the imperial architect and established a series of rules for new building activity in the city. The old limitations on the buildings of non-Muslims within the city neighborhoods were lifted. The width of the roads, number of floors, and limitations on the additional parts of houses were set by this office following standards established in Europe. Although the applications on old parts of the city were limited, the new neighborhoods reflected these changes. New ministries, banks, consulates, schools, hotels, clock towers, police stations, train stations, and apartment buildings were built. These new buildings, which were built in the European manner in plan and decoration often by European architects, gave Istanbul a feeling of the European cities. Among the surviving examples of these buildings is the first museum building (the present

Archaeological Museum of Istanbul) built in 1891, the first train station built in 1887 in Sirkeci, the first medical school in Haydarpaşa (presently serving as Marmara University) built in 1893-1903, and the Botter apartments in Pera. The European baroque, neo-classic, neo-baroque, and art nouveu styles have been used in various degrees in an eclectic manner in the architecture of the period.

Decorative arts

The decorative arts of the period are generally referred to as the Turkish rococo since the garlands, baskets, and ribbons that are dominant in the French rococo are generously used at the expense of the traditional Ottoman decorative repertoire. Motifs of the neoclassical style also began to dominate 19th century Ottoman decoration in various media. New Ottoman factories for ceramics, textiles, and glass opened up to take the place of the hand industries. These factories often resorted to foreign technology. For example, Yıldız ceramic factory established by Abdülhamid II was built to supply the porcelain ware of the palace. Several workers were hired from Limoge in France and semiprocessed clay was imported from France. An Ottoman artist who was sent to Sevres to learn this art was made the chief artist for the Yıldız factory on his return. In the section below only a selective group of objects and materials are discussed to exemplify the general trends of the 19th and early 20th century and the emphasis has been on the traditional forms and media in order to show the profound changes that occurred even on these examples.

Architectural decoration

The baroque and rococo styles of Europe, which began to affect Ottoman art in the mid-18th century, were increasingly used in the 19th century. In addition, the neoclassical style garlands, draped curtains, and columns with ancient capitals

Fig. 71 Imperial council hall, Topkapı Palace Museum

began to be applied (Fig. 71 Imperial council hall, Topkapı Palace Museum). Brushwork decoration on plaster or wood completely took the place of tile decoration on Ottoman interiors. Landscapes and still-lifes, which began to be used in the 18th century, continued to be applied as well. Views of the Bosphorus and Golden Horn with contemporary buildings and steamboats, a novelty of the 19th century, began to be applied as wall paintings in a documentary way similar to the classical Ottoman historical manuscripts. There were several European artists working in Istanbul at that time. Istanbul landscapes were a common theme of their drawings and oil paintings. Ottoman artists closely followed them as well and eventually oil paintings became a medium for Ottoman artists too. Especially in the second half of the 19th century brushwork technique gave way to the oil painting technique either directly applied on wood or on a layer of canvas stretched on ceilings or walls. These oil paintings on wood or plaster in the new Ottoman palaces included antique-shaped vases, fruit baskets, hunting scenes, and other still-life themes. Towards the end

Fig. 72 Ortaköy Mosque interior

of the 19th century human figures seen from a distance also appeared in wall paintings. While the first paintings including illusionistic building interiors, a favorite theme for ceilings in Europe, were applied by European and local Christian artists in the Dolmabahçe Palace, local Ottoman artists gradually began to employ the same technique and styles as well. Many of the Ottoman palaces built after the Dolmabahçe display these novel themes of the Ottomans. In fact even the mosque interiors followed the same styles. Ortaköy Mosque built by Abdülmecid in 1854 followed the same illusionistic style in the decoration of its dome and pendentives (Fig. 72 Ortaköy Mosque interior). Here one sees all the new elements of the style the Ottomans adopted from Europe: cartouches framed by acanthus leaves, seashell motifs, saw-cut frieze, tasseled curtains that open onto an illusionistic sky seen through columns and arcades, and finally shaded rendering of the individual motifs. Not only the exteriors but the interiors of Ottoman imperial buildings displayed almost a complete break from traditional Ottoman designs.

In the second half of the 19th century the oil painting technique on walls also eventually lead to separate paintings hung on walls. Many of the first Ottoman painters were trained in the imperial military school since technical drawings were part of their curriculum. These artists applied the Istanbul landscapes common in wall paintings on smaller canvas paintings with attention to drawing and perspective. Figures were still shunned as a reflection of traditional values, although that too was eventually overcome.

An area related to architectural decoration is Ottoman tombstones. Tombstones, which were for generations decorated with the traditional motifs, were not immune to the Europeanization of their decorative program either. Garlands,

Fig. 73 Ottoman tombstone, 1856, Süleymaniye Mosque courtyard

ancient columns, vases with flowers, and acanthus scrolls came to dominate the 19th century tombstones especially of the wealthy classes. A tombstone dated to 1856 in the courtyard of the Süleymaniye Mosque (Fig. 73 Ottoman tombstone, 1856, Süleymaniye Mosque courtyard) displays in high relief the European classicizing acanthus scrolls. While Ottoman tombstones always had a sculptural side in the form of the depiction of the headgear of the deceased whether it was janissary headgear or the later 'fez' as a standing unit above the cenotaph, the 19th century tombstones made much greater use of sculptural elements not only on the headstone but also on the cenotaph itself. These standing headpieces shaped like a veil for a female or a sale for an admiral are novel applications in an Islamic context.

Works on paper and decorated manuscripts

Although the production of illustrated manuscripts, which was predominantly under the sole patronage of the court circles, more or less came to an end in the 19th century, illuminated manuscripts especially Korans continued to be made despite the introduction of the print. The baroque and rococo styles became dominant in both illumination and bindings. In fact it is known

Fig. 74 Treatise, Topkapı Palace Museum, MR 276, binding

that illuminators of this period worked as binders in the palace. The decorative vocabulary that was applied on architectural decoration was also dominant on manuscript decoration. A binding of a treatise from the Topkapı Palace collection (Fig. 74 Treatise, Topkapı Palace Museum, MR 276, binding) shows the development of classical Ottoman binding forms: the main medallion in the center has been enlarged and the four corner pieces are no longer quarter views of the middle medallion. Instead they act as a frame to the middle medallion. The stamped decoration of the classical Ottoman leather bindings is here applied in gold with a brush directly on the leather surface. Acanthus leaves and cornucopia motifs are used as the main element of the design. The Mevlevi turban, which was worn by Sufi dervishes of the Mevlevi order, is placed in the middle of the centerpiece. The use of the turban indicates the Mevlevi connection of the text. Textiles embroidered with this turban were placed as tomb covers over Mevlevis. There is almost nothing traditional on the binding except for the main center and corner pieces which are also interpreted in design and technique. An example of the changed styles of illumination can be seen on an

Fig. 75 Elifba (alphabeth book) Topkapı Palace Museum, EH435 1b-2a

Palace Museum, EH435 1b-2a). Mustafa Vasıf (d. 1852), who was an important calligrapher of the period, copied the letters. The first two pages are illuminated with the common style of the period. Flower bouquets, ribbons, and acanthus leaves are symmetrically arranged around the text block like a frame. In addition the pink, purple and emerald green colors do not show any resemblance to the color combinations of classical Ottoman illumination.

Calligraphy continued as a separate art form as printing took the place of copying. Calligraphic panels became a common area for the calligraphers to apply their art. An interesting transformation of the *Hilye* perhaps best reflects the profound changes of Ottoman society.

Hilye is a sort of calligraphic design in which the physical appearance, character, manners, and ethics of the Prophet Muhammad are described in words. A round medallion is used for this description. In the four corners of this medallion names of the first four caliphs are placed. Although *hilyes* were written on paper as in other Islamic countries the famed Ottoman calligrapher Hafiz Osman (1642-1698) wrote *hilyes* on small panels. Later in the mid-19th century another calligrapher Kazasker Mustafa Izzet (1801-1876) enlarged this form and Hasan Rıza (1849-1920), who was one of the leading calligraphers of the early 20th century, extended it to sizes reaching two meters by including an additional text. Some of the *hilyes* were also illustrated with the images of Mecca and Medina on top of the text as well. In this example by Hasan Rıza dated to 1905 (Fig. 76 *Hilye*, Sakıp Sabancı Museum, 140-0113 HR) beyond the usual division of the written text, the floral decorations that fill the empty zones display the typical decoration of the period. The circular medallion in the middle is surrounded with garlands creating a crescent shape. Flowers set in vases are placed on the sides. Voluminous floral scrolls

Fig. 76 Hilye, Sakıp Sabancı Museum, 140-0113 HR

and bouquets of roses which symbolize the prophet Muhammad are spread in the remaining areas. The main frame is decorated with stylized cornucopia motifs used like a floral scroll. At the bottom "If it were not for you I, God, would not have created the heavens" is inscribed referring to the Prophet Muhammad in large *sülüs* to enlarge the *hilye* proper. The text between the two large lines of calligraphy also refers to the Prophet and copies the 107th verse of the Koran common for this section: "We have only sent you to be a blessing to the universe". The height of the frame is a little over a meter (107x74cm). Hasan Rıza Efendi (1849-1920), who taught calligraphy in various schools, copied several Korans and a *hilye* for Sultan Mehmed V Reşad (1909-18). One of his Korans was printed several times as well.

These large *hilyes* were used to decorate large mansions, which were built in numbers during the 19th century. As the idea of hanging paintings on walls penetrated into the Ottoman interiors, *hilyes* came to be used in the same manner. Since on *hilyes* the face of the Prophet Muhammed is 'painted' in words, the hanging *hilye* must have found a receptive environment for the wealthy but perhaps more conservative Muslims of Ottoman society. According to a saying of the Prophet (*hadith*) those in a house with a *hilye* would be protected from robbers, genies, the devil, illnesses, magic and spells, and no fire would harm such a house. This added protective element must have also resulted in the wider use of *hilye* panels.

Chapter 9

Bibliography

16. Yüzyıl Osmanlı Kültür ve Sanatı: 11-12 Nisan 2001, sempozyum bildirileri. Istanbul, 2004.

17. Yüzyıl Osmanlı Kültür ve Sanatı: 19-20 Mart 1998, sempozyum bildirileri. Istanbul, 1998.

The Anatolian Civilizations, Seljuk/Ottoman. N. Tapan, S. Aykoç and F. Çağman, exh. cat. Ferit Edgü (ed.). Istanbul, 1983.

Aslanapa, Oktay. *Osmanlı Devri Mimarisi: Orhan Gaziden başlayarak sonuna kadar padişahlara göre gelişmesi*. Istanbul, 1986.

Atasoy, Nurhan. *Surname-i Hümayun, 1582: An Imperial Celebration*. Istanbul, 1997.

Atasoy, Nurhan, and Julian Raby. *Iznik: The Pottery of Ottoman Turkey*. London, 1989.

Atasoy, Nurhan, Julian Jaby, and Alison Effeny. *Ipek: The Crescent and the Rose: Ottoman Imperial Silks and Velvets*. London, 2001.

Atasoy, Nurhan, and Tülay Artan. *Splendors of the Ottoman Sultans*. Memphis, Tenn., 1992.

Atıl, Esin. *Süleymanname: The Illustrated History of Süleyman the Magnificent*. Washington, D.C., 1986.

Atıl, Esin. *The Age of Sultan Süleyman the Magnificent*. Washington, D.C., 1987.

Bağcı, Serpil, Filiz Çağman, Günsel Renda, and Zeren Tanındı. *Osmanlı Resim Sanatı*. Istanbul, 2006.

Bilgi, Hülya. *Dance of Fire: Iznik Tiles and Ceramics in the Sadberk Hanım Museum and Ömer M. Koç Collections*. Istanbul, 2009.

Bilgi, Hülya. *Çatma ve Kemha: Osmanlı İpekli Dokumaları = Çatma & Kemha: Ottoman Silk Textiles*. Istanbul, 2007.

Çağman, Filiz. "The Ahmed Karahisari Qur'an" *Persian Painting: From the Mongols to the Qajars: Studies in Honour of Basil W. Robinson*. Robert Hillenbrand and Basil W. Robinson (eds.). London, 2000.

Çağman, Filiz, and Zeren Tanındı. *The Topkapı Saray Museum: The Albums and Illustrated manuscripts*. J. Michael Rogers (ed. and trans.). London, 1987.

Çağman, Filiz, and Hülya Tezcan. *Topkapı Palace*. Istanbul, 2000.

Cezar, Mustafa. *Osmanlı Başkenti İstanbul*. Istanbul, 2002.

Denny, Walter B. *The Artistry of Ottoman Ceramics*. London, 2004.

Derman, M. Uğur. *Letters in Gold: Ottoman Calligraphy from the Sakıp Sabancı Collection*, New York, 1998.

Duran, Gülnur. *Ali Üsküdârî: tezhip ve ruganî üstâdı, çiçek ressamı*. Istanbul, 2008.

Eldem, Edhem. *Death in Istanbul: Death and Its Rituals in Ottoman-Islamic Culture*. Istanbul, 2005.

Goodwin, Godfrey. *A History of Ottoman Architecture*. London, 1987.

Hamadeh, Shirine. *The City's Pleasures: Istanbul in the Eighteenth Century*. Seattle, 2008.

İnalcık, Halil. *1300 – 1600: An economic and social history of the Ottoman Empire*. Cambridge, 1999.

İnalcık, Halil, and Günsel Renda. (eds.) *Ottoman Civilization*. Ankara, 2003.

Köseoğlu, Cengiz. *Topkapı: The Treasury*. J. Michael Rogers (trans. and ed.). London, 1987.

Kuban, Doğan. *Ottoman Architecture*. Istanbul, 2005.

Labrusse, Rémi. *Purs décors?: arts de l'Islam, regards du XIX. siècle; collections des Arts Décoratifs*. Paris, 2007.

Mantran, Robert. *Histoire de l'empire Ottoman*. Paris, 1989.

Necipoğlu, Gülru. "A Kanun for the State, a Canon for the Arts: Conceptualizing the Classical Synthesis of Ottoman Art and Architecture," in *Soliman le Magnifique et son temps*, edited by Gilles Veinstein. Paris, 1992, pp. 194-216.

Necipoğlu, Gülru. *The Age of Sinan: Architectural Culture in the Ottoman Empire*. Princeton, 2005.

Necipoğlu, Gülru. *Architecture, Ceremonial, and Power: The Topkapı Palace in the Fifteenth and Sixteenth Centuries*. New York, 1991.

Necipoğlu, Gülru. "From International Timurid to Ottoman: A change of taste in sixteenth-century ceramic tiles" *Muqarnas* 7 (1990): pp. 136-70.

Öney, Gönül, and Zehra Çobanlı. *Anadolu'da Türk Devri Çini ve Seramik Sanatı*. Ankara, 2007.

Raby, Julian, and Zeren Tanındı. *Turkish Bookbinding in the Fifteenth Century: The Foundation of an Ottoman court style*. London, 1993.

Rogers, J. M., and R. M. Ward. *Süleyman the Magnificent*. London, 1988.

Roxburgh, David J. (ed.) *Turks: a journey of a thousand years, 600-1600*. London, 2005.

Sakaoğlu, Necdet. *Bu Mülkün Sultanları: 36 Osmanlı Padişahı.* Istanbul, 1999.

Tezcan, Hülya, and Selma Delibaş. *Topkapı Textiles*. J. Michael Rogers (trans. and ed.). London, 1986.

Topkapı Sarayı Müzesi, and Musée national des châteaux de Versailles et de Trianon. *Topkapi à Versailles: trésors de la cour ottomane*. Paris, 1999.

Veinstein, Gilles. (ed). *Soliman le Magnifique et son temps*. Paris, 1992.